THE CUTTIN(
S E L F – S T

Sales &
Service

Christel F. Land, MBA

Foreword by Cesare Carcano

To Karen and Steven,

the first two people
to teach me about business.

Contents

Foreword
by Cesare Carcano

Everything I do in my life is based on my personal paradigm: Vision, Consistency and Choice.

Vision: I always have to have a wide view of where I want to go. It's not merely a matter of having a strategy or a goal. Vision is a broader context in which each of our actions has to face the reactions of the environment around us.

Consistency: I need to always make sure that my vision, even if a fully creative one, is not just a fun dream.

Choice: If Vision is based on Consistency, I then have a good chance of making the right Choice, and therefore being on the right path!

Christel Land is all of this!

She's Vision. Thanks to her extraordinary professional experience in the self-storage world, she knows how to identify successful yet easy-to-follow paths which can be followed by anyone.

She's Consistency. Each of her pieces of advice are based on cutting edge and widely documented knowledge.

She's Choice. She allows us to make specific choices to improve our performance in a precise and sustainable way.

In the self-storage industry, the quality of the relationship we can create with our customer undoubtedly represents the main key to success. It's not a matter of speaking, kindness or achieving incredible conversion rates. It's a matter of changing our perspective from 'we rent space' to 'we understand our customer'.

Christel Land's book is the right tool to start this journey. Step by step, in a detailed yet simple way, the book provides us with practical tools to become better sales experts, to understand our customers' personality in detail and to be able to manage critical issues as well as to create loyalty.

'Sales & Service' is already a best seller. Not because it's a unique professional manual for those in sales, but rather for its practicality: it can be read by anyone who deals with customers and discussed with your best friends too.

Cesare Carcano

CEO & Owner
Casaforte Self-Storage Group, Italy

A Great Thing

"Great things are done by a series of small things brought together."

Vincent Van Gogh

The difference between the good and the great is often much smaller than we think. It can be tempting to think that the best companies in the world or the best performers in our field are doing something completely different to ourselves.

In reality, they are not.

After 13 years in the self-storage industry and over a decade as a business coach and consultant in a variety of industries, I have seen many examples of trajectories changing. Growth of entire businesses and growth of individuals within those businesses.

What they all have in common is that the change in trajectory, the change in results, hasn't come from big, radical changes. It hasn't happened by throwing everything up in the air and letting it land in completely new places.

It has been my experience that the most solid path to growth is one of fine-tuning and being very deliberate in everything that is done. Breaking things down into pieces and looking at how that individual little piece can be perfected.

Spotting potential is about seeing greatness in the smallest of places. Achieving potential is about identifying how each part of the whole can be perfected, and then taking action to make those changes. When many small changes like that are compounded together, that is when trajectories change.

That is also why I decided to write this book.

As a business coach, my clients rely on me to stay on top of the latest research, trends and best practices. Especially in the field of psychology and neuroscience, there have been some amazing advances over the past 15 years. These are advances that offer very practical lessons in how we can get better results when we are selling and serving our customers.

As I go around the self-storage industry advising different businesses, I see time and time again that these new discoveries haven't been incorporated into the way we market, sell and serve. That is the reason I decided to write this book; to combine the most relevant research with industry know-how and best practices, in order to help propel the industry forward.

When you read through this book, you will notice that I am not offering a radically different approach to sales and service. What I am offering is a very deliberate attention to the details you need to master, if you want to make the most of every customer interaction you have.

Vincent Van Gogh said that "great things are done by a series of small things brought together". This book offers you those many small things, so that you can adapt it to your own circumstances and create a great thing. So that you can change your trajectory.

May it leave you inspired,

Christel

The Selling Mindset

"If you think you can do a thing or you think you can't do a thing, you're right."

Henry Ford

Is Selling A Dirty Word?

Imagine that you are going into a shop of some kind and a salesperson comes over and starts talking to you. What are the first three words that spring to your mind to describe that salesperson?

This little exercise is what I have found to be the quickest way to learn what someone's mindset is around sales.

The answers I get when I ask this question vary a lot. Some people say predominantly positive words like helpful, knowledgeable and listening. Others say predominantly negative words like pushy, arrogant and self-centered.

I have not yet met a person who would like to be pushy, arrogant or self-centered. I haven't run in to someone who says: "I'd like to work on being a bit more arrogant". Those aren't qualities we as human beings aspire towards.

That is why it makes perfect sense that if we instinctively and intuitively view salespeople as having those qualities, then we will struggle to feel completely comfortable being in sales ourselves. Oftentimes, people who feel this way will be comfortable saying they work with sales but will never spontaneously describe themselves as a salesperson.

That is why our exploration of sales starts with the mind. Our perspective or mindset on something determines a lot in how our lives unfold, and sales is no exception. The perspective we take, consciously or unconsciously, can trip us up or propel us forward. We are going to look now at how you can use your mind to propel you forward in sales.

You Are Doing It Already!

The place to start to de-dramatize sales is to acknowledge that the skills we use when we are selling, are skills that we use in other walks of life all the time. We ask questions, we help others solve problems, we strike up conversations with people we don't know, or set an appointment for doing something important. If you think back to the past seven days of your life, there is a decent chance you have done all of these. We are constantly using the skills we use in sales, just in different contexts.

And yet when we use those skills in sales, it can suddenly feel different. That change in how we feel is often caused by something known as limiting beliefs.

Limiting Beliefs

Limiting beliefs are beliefs that we hold, and that limit us in some way. In the example from earlier, if we view salespeople as pushy and arrogant and we have just taken our first job in sales, we might have a hard time succeeding on the job. Because who wants to be pushy and arrogant? So, as you read through this book try to notice if you have any limiting beliefs around sales yourself.

If you do notice any limiting beliefs, there is a simple way to work on changing those beliefs, so they don't trip you up as you develop your own sales skills:

1. Acknowledge that it is a belief and not the absolute truth.

2. Create an empowering belief to replace your limiting belief.

3. Find evidence of your new, empowering belief.

4. Repeat until your belief has changed.

If until now you have seen salespeople as arrogant and self-centered, then that would be the limiting belief. An empowering belief to replace it could be that salespeople are helpful instead.

As you go around your daily life you could start noticing all the different ways that salespeople are actually being really helpful towards you. That would be one way of finding evidence of your new, empowering belief. If you kept doing this, then over time your belief would change.

If this sounds like it is easier said than done, then you are absolutely right. It is easier said than done. But it is also rarely as difficult as we think it will be before we start. As the quote from Henry Ford at the beginning of this chapter says: "If you think you can do a thing or you think you can't do a thing, you're right".

The Most Common Limiting Belief in Self-Storage Sales

By far the most common limiting belief that I run in to as I work with self-storage companies of different sizes and in different markets, is about how price sensitive our customers are.

I see time and time again that those of us working in self-storage sales believe that our customers are more price sensitive than they actually are. And there is a really simple reason why that is.

When potential customers call or visit a facility, a lot of them will open up the conversation something like this:

"I need storage at the end of the month, and I am just calling/visiting to ask how much it costs."

It is very common for customers to open up a conversation asking about price. So, as salespeople we hear questions of price over and over again. It is only natural then, that over time we start thinking that our customers care a lot about price. After all, that is all they really seem to be asking us about.

The thing is, self-storage is a product that most customers don't know a lot of technical information about. They don't know that units can have different heights or that doors can have different widths. They don't know that there are different access hours to choose from or that some units might have individual door alarms. Most customers don't know a lot of technical information about self-storage, so they ask the only question that makes sense to them; how much does it cost?

I hope that this awareness can help you to not fall into the trap of believing that all customers care about is price, even if that is what they will ask you about the most. Yes, customers care about price. But they care about other stuff too, and they don't care as much about price as we tend to think they do.

So, the next time you hear that question, try to avoid the temptation to translate it in to 'the most important thing to my customer is price'. Try instead to translate it in to 'they aren't sure what to ask about and are trying to start a storage conversation with me'.

What Is Selling Actually?

Whether you are new to sales or you already have experience, it can be helpful to take a moment to find your own definition of what sales is.

The definition of sales that this book is based on is this:

Sales is helping other people buy.

It is about using our knowledge about self-storage, using good questions and good people skills to understand exactly what the customer is looking for. And then to help them make the best buying decision for them.

Because the truth of the matter is that as much as we would like to, as salespeople we just don't know what is right for the customer. Only the customer knows that. Our role is to help them buy and to make sure they have all the right information and guidance along the way.

That is why I think of sales training mostly as people training. It is also the reason you will find a heap of references in this book to neuroscience and to the field of psychology. Mastering sales is first and foremost about being good at people.

Dealing with Rejection

When we see sales this way, it also helps us deal with one of the biggest obstacles in sales; the fear of rejection.

Unless your conversion rate is 100% all the time, I can guarantee that you will experience rejection in sales. In fact, if your conversion rate is 40%, you will hear 'no' 1.5 times more often than you will hear 'yes'. Hearing 'no' from our potential customers comes with the territory of sales, so how can we feel okay about it?

When we see sales as helping other people buy, then it naturally helps us deal with rejection. That is because we are clearly separating you as a salesperson from the outcome of the sale.

Our role as salespeople is to make the most of every enquiry that comes our way. Our job is to show potential customers how we are the right solution to their problem. But if the customer decides not to rent from us, they are not rejecting us as people. They are rejecting what we offer. They are simply saying 'right now, this is not right for me'.

Growing

There are two more aspects of the selling mindset that are important to our success in sales; continuous learning and goal setting.

We are going to take a closer look at both of those when we get towards the end of this books. In the chapter 'Growing', we will look at how you can stay successful in sales over time.

Before we do that though, we will dive deeper in to how we become successful in the first place. That starts with learning about the Spiral of Sales.

The Doggy Bag on Mindset

o How you see salespeople in general will influence your own success in sales.

o The skills we use in sales are skills we use in other walks of life on a daily basis.

o Identify any limiting beliefs that you have around sales.

o To change a limiting belief, you will need to replace it with an empowering belief and find evidence of that new belief.

o When your customer asks you about price, it doesn't mean they are hugely price sensitive. It may simply mean they are trying to start a conversation with you about something they know very little about.

o In this book, sales is defined as helping other people buy.

o Rejection is a natural part of working in sales. To deal with this rejection, you will need to separate yourself from what you are offering.

The Spiral of Sales

"People do not care how much you know until they know how much you care."

Teddy Roosevelt

A Bit Like A Bake Sale

There is no shortage of sales models in the world. But it can be tricky to find one that is both simple and all-encompassing. A truly useful model is one we can remember in the heat of the moment, but also one that covers every part of our interaction with our customer.

As I started to train and coach people in sales, this is what I missed; a model that was simple but not simplistic. That is how the Spiral of Sales was born.

The Spiral of Sales is my own contribution to the sales models of this world. It is a model that keeps things both simple and practical, whilst providing us with clear guidance through the whole sales process.

The Spiral of Sales consists of four parts:

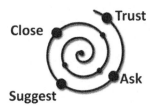

You can easily remember these parts by the first letter in each word: **T-A-S-C.**

Think of these parts as ingredients rather than clearly defined steps. If you were baking a cake, you would need a list of ingredients to make your cake tasty. In the same way, the Spiral of Sales offers you four ingredients that you need to make a sale and to make it well.

At the beginning of a sale it is more about building trust and towards the end it is more about closing. But all four parts are interacting with each other throughout the sale.

Hang On, Is It Really That Simple?

But wait, selling doesn't usually go that easily, right? What if the customer says 'no' or gives us some kind of objection?

Objection handling needs a process of its own and that process happens to be exactly the same as what comes before the 'no'.

When we get an objection, we need to confirm trust with the customer. We need to ask clarifying questions and suggest another perspective on their objection. And then, we need to try to close them again.

That is why this model is called the Spiral of Sales and not the Circle of Sales. For each objection we get, we go one more time around the circle. But each time we do, we close the circle tighter and tighter until we end up at the final close.

We are now going to dive into each part of the Spiral of Sales to discover how we can master each of them.

The Spiral of Sales

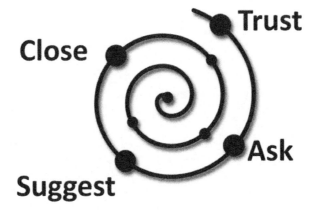

Trust

"To be trusted is a greater compliment than being loved."
George MacDonald

When Is the Last Time You Did A Trust Audit?

The first part of our Spiral of Sales is trust. It is the foundation of long-term, sustainable business growth and it should be a cornerstone of any sales process.

Trust is difficult to measure though. There is no straightforward way to tell us exactly how we are doing in the area of trust. Maybe that is why it tends to get less airtime in our day-to-day activities. Instead, we end up focusing more on things that are easier to measure through KPIs and targets.

So, I hope I can inspire you to do a trust audit in your own site or business. Start with your sales process and after that, look at all your touchpoints with customers, from move-in to move-out and beyond. For each of these steps and each of your activities, score yourself on trustworthiness.

Once your results are in, you will have a clear picture of where you can improve individual parts of your sales or service processes. By doing this regularly, you can be sure to leave your customers feeling like they are renting from a trustworthy business.

Why Trust Matters

There has been heaps of research done on what happens in our brains when we are buying. What we know from this research is that one of the strongest psychological forces at play when we buy something, is a force known as loss aversion. In other words, we want to avoid experiencing loss.

In fact, if we compare loss with its opposite of joy, our emotional reaction to loss is actually <u>twice</u> as intense as when we feel happy.[i]

That is why loss aversion is one of the strongest psychological factors that we are up against when we are selling. So, of course the next question follows naturally from that; how can we reduce the customer's sense of risk or loss?

In 2001, the Nobel Prize in Economics went to George Akerlof. One of the things his research revealed is that trust is the single most effective way to reduce a customer's sense of risk.[ii] And that is why trust matters so much when we are selling.

What is the Effect of Trust?

One of the best descriptions I have found on the simple effects of trust is this: [iii]

↑Trust ↑Speed ↓Cost

↓Trust ↓Speed ↑Cost

When trust is high, things move along quicker and cost less. And when trust is low, things take longer and cost more.

If you have ever experienced a big organizational change in your company, you will have a first-hand account of this principle. Those types of situations tend to really unearth what the real trust levels are within a business.

But there are examples of this to be found in much simpler places too. Consider for a moment referral customers.

They contact you because they have heard from a friend or a relative that you are a reliable place to store their stuff. What your KPIs will probably reveal is that referral customers move through the sales process quicker and thereby cost you less. It takes less of your time to sell to them and they also cost less in the sense that you haven't had to market to them. Your customer has done your marketing for you, completely for free!

The Expectations Game

So, we have established that trust is important. But how do we do it? How do we build trust with our customers?

It is actually quite simple to do but it can still be a challenge, especially as teams and businesses grow. That is because trust is about setting our customers' expectations and then delivering consistently on those expectations. It is about all of us operating in the same way and speaking with one voice.

Trust is about saying what we are going to do and then following through and doing exactly that. Not every once in a while, not in most cases, but every single time. And it is the every-single-time-part that can be a challenge as a company grows and evolves.

That is the reason why it is so important to have a clearly defined sales process.

It is also why we need a system of some kind that will prompt us to do exactly what we have said we are going to do. As soon as we are juggling more than a handful of leads at a time, we need some form of outside help to ensure that we deliver on every single promise we make, no matter how small it may be.

On a very practical level, a great way to build trust is to always finish one step of the sales process by telling the customer what the next step will be. That could go something like this:

"After we hang up, I'll send you an email with all the reservation details that we have spoken about today. And then I'll give you a call two days before you move in, just to check if you have any questions we need to clear up before you come down here."

By consistently doing that throughout the sales process, we are being explicit about setting the customer's expectations. By telling them exactly what to expect, we are leaving little or no room for them to set those expectations themselves, out of thin air.

What we are also doing is showing our customer that we follow through on what we say we are going to do, every single step of the way. It is absolutely true that actions speak louder than words. That is why this one small sales habit goes a long way to showing our customers that we can be trusted.

Be Personal, Be Sincere

Think back to the last time you went out to buy something, where you encountered a salesperson who you didn't really like at all. Maybe their style was very different to yours? Maybe they seemed uninterested? Maybe they were too keen to serve?

Now think of that buying decision you made and whether your feelings towards the salesperson influenced you in any way. Without being able to read your mind right now, my guess is your answer to that question is "yes".

It has been shown time and time again that as customers, we are more likely to buy from people we can identify with and that we like. Likability is a big factor in determining who we end up buying from[iv] and this has two main implications when we are selling.

The first one is that people don't only buy from a business, they also buy from a person. As a business grows, sales can tend to get less personal and that can lead to missed opportunities when we are selling. As customers, we are subjected to so much marketing and buying in our daily lives. This makes us very astute to notice when we are dealing with someone who is just following a process, instead of sincerely caring about helping us. So, when you are selling, show them the person they are buying from!

The second implication of likability is one that we have a whole section about in this book. Different customers have different 'currencies' for trust. Some customers want to have a long chat with you, while others will want to head straight for the door if you are too talkative with them.

So, the better you can get at spotting which customer type you are dealing with and knowing how you should adapt your style to them, the better you will get at building trust.

Know Your Stuff

The more you can show your customer that you are the expert on storage, the more they will trust you. The way to do that is first and foremost to know your stuff in terms of estimating space, what units you have available, and so on.

Showing your customer that you are the expert is also just as much about challenging your customer's thinking about storage when they speak to you.

An interesting study[v] on sales looked at how different sales styles impacted result. Conventional wisdom on sales tells us that the better we are at building relationships, the better we will be at selling. This study showed that this isn't actually the case at all! The salespeople who get the best results are the ones who are able to challenge the customer's thinking as they sell to them.

Challenging our customer's thinking can often take the form of sharing space saving tips with them. So, tell them as much as you can about how to make the most of their space!

And if you are a manager with a team, don't just leave space saving tips as something that comes with experience. Make it something that your team is trained on. Make it an integrated part of your sales scripts, sales training and sales process.

Hand on Heart

In order to build trust, a lot of businesses offer guarantees of some kind. But whether a guarantee actually helps us sell can vary a lot. And there is a very simple explanation to why that is.

The most powerful guarantees are put together in response to whatever your customers' number one objection is when they buy from you.

So, if the most common objection you get from your customers is around price, then a price guarantee will be effective for you. If instead your most common objection is that they want to speak to their husband or wife before they decide, you might find a guarantee like this to be more effective:

"We guarantee that your spouse will love our storage facility. If he or she doesn't - for whatever reason - then your next dinner out will be on us."

You can have a bit of fun with this and turn it in to something that puts a smile on your customer's face.

No matter what your guarantee is, its effectiveness will depend on whether or not it has been matched to your customers' objections. If you can get creative and stand out from your competition in the way you present it, then it will work even better.

The Art of Un-Selling

Un-selling starts with the acknowledgement that perfect isn't believable. And perfect isn't trustworthy. If all we hear from a salesperson is how wonderful everything is, we automatically start wondering what it is they are <u>not</u> telling us.

Un-selling is when we openly share something with our customer that isn't perfect about our business. This is something that can feel counter-intuitive to salespeople and it is a technique that we need to use skillfully. Whatever imperfections we share with the customer should of course not work against us when it is time to close the sale.

Un-selling can be something as simple as mentioning that a button in an elevator can be temperamental and needs a stronger push or telling them that traffic to your site is usually heavy in the late afternoon.

What NOT to Do

I have done quite a lot of mystery shopping for self-storage companies, which is really good fun. One of the things I have noticed during these experiences is so common that it deserves a separate mention here.

Some salespeople, especially the ones who don't feel completely comfortable selling, tend to tell several personal stories in the sales conversation. They tell stories about what it was like when they needed storage themselves. They do this with the best of intentions; to build trust and rapport by showing the customer that they can relate to their situation.

Personal stories can absolutely have a place in a sales conversation. It can be one way of showing our customer who it is they are dealing with. But they need to be kept really short.

As customers we are inherently self-centered. That is why personal stories should only be used if they contain some piece of advice that will help your customer in some way. If you tell a story just for the sake of telling a story, chances are you will lose their interest and their attention.

So, if you or your colleagues have been building trust by using several personal references in your selling, try dialing these back a little. Try replacing them with some of the other ways to build trust that we have just covered. You will find that your customer stays interested for longer and is more likely to buy from you.

The Doggy Bag on Trust

o   Trust matters. Always.

o   Do a trust audit in your site or business to identify places where you can signal more trust to your customers.

o   Have a clearly defined sales process that identifies stages and actions.

o   Have systems in place to prompt for any actions that are needed, both for sales and for service.

o   Learn how to spot and sell to different customer types.

o   Know your stuff so well that you can challenge your customer's thinking about their storage needs.

o   Match your company guarantee with your most common sales objection.

o   Add un-selling to your arsenal of sales techniques.

o   Keep personal stories to a minimum and if you include them, relate them to advice that can help your customer.

Ask

"A prudent question is one-half of wisdom."
Francis Bacon

Our Anatomy Gives Us A Clue

The second part of our Spiral of Sales is about asking good questions. One of the best pieces of sales advice I ever got was this:

"We have two ears and one mouth. Use them in proportion."

In other words, we should listen twice as much as we speak. And good listening starts by asking good questions.

So, what makes a question good when we are selling?

Getting in the Mood

To answer that, we need to understand how we get a customer in the mood to buy. That starts with understanding a few things about how our brains work.

Customers who are in a positive state of mind are much more likely to buy. In fact, there are studies that show that even something as simple as the weather actually has a great impact on how we feel and consequently, how likely we are to buy something.[vi]

We also know from neuroscience that our brains can actually only focus on one thing at a time; our brains actually can't multitask.[vii] That means that the way we ask our questions will directionalize our customer's mind.

As such, we can influence whether the customer's mind is directonalized to a more positive state (which helps us sell) or to a more negative state (which is a roadblock to selling).

Imagine you are walking around your storage facility with a future customer and you ask them a conversational question. You could ask them any one of these three questions:

"Have you arranged everything for your move yet?"

"Is it a busy time for you during your move?"

"What will you do with the extra space you have at home after you move?"

If we ask the first two questions, we are directionalizing our customer's mind towards a slightly stressed state. We are tuning them in to their to-do-lists, which are likely to be long.

In the third question we are directionalizing our customer's mind towards why it is all worth it; what their new home will be like after the move is done.

There is something else that tends to put our brains in a good mood for buying and that is the simple joy of saying 'yes' to something. As human beings we find it much more pleasant to say 'yes' to something, than to say 'no' to something. In fact, one of the age-old tricks in sales is to get people to say yes to small things throughout the sales process. Once they reach the final close, they are then more likely to say yes to that one too.

So, we are now ready to start answering what makes a question good when we are selling. A good question in sales is first and foremost a question that will put our customer in a more positive state of mind and a question that they can say 'yes' to.

Open or Closed?

A good question in sales is also well-timed. Yes, timing is everything and sales is no exception.

There are lots of different ways to categorize questions and this is something that sales books tend to love to dive into. At its most practical and fundamental level, you only need to categorize questions in two groups; open questions and closed questions.

Open questions are questions that wouldn't naturally be answered with a simple one-word answer like 'yes' or 'no'. These are questions that prompt some kind of conversational answer instead.

Closed questions are the exact opposite. These are questions that can be answered with a simple one-word answer.

For a sales conversation to flow as naturally as possible you should start it off with open questions. Then as the conversation progresses, you move in to closed questions.

A questioning sequence that would make for a naturally flowing conversation could consist of these questions in this order:

1. Why do you need storage? *(open)*

2. What do you need to put in storage? *(open)*

3. Have you ever used self-storage before? *(open / closed)*

4. When do you need storage? *(closed)*

5. How long do you need storage for? *(closed)*

To contrast that, try playing out this next questioning sequence in your mind and imagine how the conversation would go:

1. How long do you need storage for? *(closed)*

2. When do you need storage? *(closed)*

3. Have you ever used self-storage before? *(open/closed)*

4. Why do you need storage? *(open)*

5. What do you need to put in storage? *(open)*

You would probably find it much harder to get a natural conversation going by asking your questions in this order.

So, as a simple rule of thumb, build your sales process and sales script up in a way where you start off with open questions and finish off with more closed questions.

Do You Check How Clued Up Your Customer Is?

Consumer habits have changed a lot over the past decades and one of the big drivers in that has been the internet. We now have so much information at our fingertips and we are not afraid to use it!

One of the consequences of that has been that our customers do much more research before they ever contact us about what they need.

In fact, joint research by Google and Gartner showed that 57% of our customers' research for a buying decision happens before they ever contact a company about what they need.[viii] That's right, 57% of a sale happens away from you and the other salespeople on your team.

So, with this in mind, have your sales processes and scripts adapted to this change in how we buy?

When we speak to future customers, they are likely to be much more clued up about our company, our offering and their own needs, than they were 15-20 years ago. That is true even for customers who have never used self-storage before.

That is why it is a good idea to check how much your customer knows as soon as possible in the conversation. Maybe they already have some specific questions in mind about what you offer? We want to be sure to uncover all this before we leap into a standardized sales script and questioning sequence.

Building in some variety of these next questions into your sales process is a simple way to achieve that:

"Have you visited our website?"

"Is there anything from there that you want me to go in to detail about, as we speak about what size storage unit you will need?"

So, a good question in sales is also one that takes in to account the fact that your customer is much more clued up than they used to be.

Adding Extra Spice

Most self-storage companies cross-sell different products and services; moving boxes, packing materials, padlocks, insurances and van rentals, just to mention a few.

Extras usually represent a pretty easy way to bump up our margin and our average value sale by a nice amount. That is why there is every reason to build extras in as a completely natural part of the conversation we have about storage.

Some self-storage companies treat the extras as a completely separate sale. These companies tend to find that the income they generate from extras is at the lower end. The self-storage companies that I have seen who really rock the extras, do so by treating it all as one big sale.

They don't see their sales goal as only selling storage space. Instead, their goal is to put together a package for the customer that contains the space and all the extras that the customer needs.

A simple way to make your customer aware of the extras you offer is to ask a question like this early on in the conversation:

"Do you want me to give you a price only for the storage, or should I also give you a price for handling the whole move for you?"

or

"Do you want me to give you a price only for the storage, or should I also give you a price for our complete business package where we do all your delivery handling for you too?"

This is a subtle way of letting your customer know that you do extras. Since you are asking them for permission to give details on your other services, you are also turning cross-selling into something that isn't pushy. After all, you are only going to tell them about extras if they say it is okay for you to do so.

What to Ask Yourself

So far, we have been talking about questions to ask your customer. What is equally important is which questions you are asking yourself, as you are selling.

In self-storage sales, there are four questions you should be keeping at the back of your mind, as you talk your customer through their storage needs. You might not always find the answer to them. But if you can find the answer you will be able to fine-tune your approach much more when you are selling.

One: Who Is Your Competition?

By competition I don't just mean other self-storage operators. Your competition is anything that will solve the customer's problem for them. That means that your competition could be container storage or warehouse storage. It could be a friend's garage. It could even be re-arranging the move or the business startup so that the customer doesn't need storage at all.

If you can work out what your customer is comparing you to, you will be able to tailor your pitch much more skillfully. It will allow you to highlight the differences between options and show your customer all the reasons why you are the better choice.

Two: What Is Your Customer's Elephant?

Imagine that every time a customer walks through your door, they are riding on an invisible elephant. Bear with me, this metaphor does carry an important lesson for sales!

All you see is your customer, but what you can't see is the elephant they are riding on. That elephant consists of all the perceived risks and other reasons why the customer might not be prepared to buy from you.

The elephant is invisible for a reason; customers typically won't tell us what their elephant consists of. But if we can work it out as we speak to them, we will once again be able to tailor our approach. We will be able to give them arguments and assurances for why the elephant should take a walk outside and leave your customer with you to sign the rental agreement.

Three: What Makes Your Customer Smile?

Some customers are influenced heavily by objective evidence, facts and figures. Other customers are influenced more by personal assurances or stories about people who were just like them and who decided to rent from you.

As you learn how to spot and adapt to different customer types, you will learn how to determine what makes each customer type smile. As you start mastering those skills, you will be able to give each customer the kind of sales arguments that influences them the most.

Four: Will They Store Prohibited Goods?

If your customer mentions storing fireworks for New Year's Eve or that their pet snake needs a place to hang out while they go on holiday, a big red flag should be popping up in your mind.

I actually had a customer once who did just that; he put his tropical, venomous snake in his storage unit while he went on holiday. We would have never noticed, except the snake got hungry and snuck out of its terrarium.

Luckily, it was someone on my team who spotted the snake slithering down a corridor, instead of a customer. We called a special police unit to remove the snake and everyone walked away from episode unharmed and with quite a story to tell. This snake of ours even landed us a spot on the evening news that day.

So, take it from someone who has been there and done that. You can't do anything about customers who aren't honest with you. If they are intending to break the terms of the rental agreement, they probably will. But you can keep your ears and eyes open for any hints they give you about using the unit in a way that it wasn't intended for.

The Doggy Bag on Asking Questions

○ We have two ears and one mouth. Use them in proportion.

○ Customers are more likely to buy when they are in a positive state of mind, so tailor your questions to directionalize your customer to a positive state.

○ To get a natural conversation going, ask open questions at the start of a conversation and closed questions towards the end.

○ Find a way to temperature check how much research your customer has done about you before they contacted you.

○ Treat storage and any extras you sell as one big sale, rather than several separate sales.

○ Work out what your customer is comparing you to, so you can highlight all the reasons why you are the better choice.

○ Work out what your customer's elephant is made up of and if you can, tell it to take a walk while you close the sale.

○ Listen out for any references to your customer planning to store prohibited goods in their unit.

Suggest

"A problem well put is half solved."
John Dewey

Made to Measure

Once your questions have given you a good understanding of your customer's needs and motivations, it is time for the third part of our Spiral of Sales. It is time to suggest a solution.

The golden rule to suggesting solutions is to make it as tailor-made as possible. We all know that feeling of contacting a company about one specific thing and then ending up being bombarded with all the different ways they can help us.

The key to avoiding making our customers feel like that is to make our suggestions tailor-made. Wherever you can, reference something they have told you when you explain why this solution is right for them.

This is true whether you are estimating how much space they need, where in the building will suit them or what kind of extra products and services they will need.

Going Back in Time

There is real skill to presenting a solution to a customer in a way that makes them want to buy from us. To master that skill, we first need to take a short leap back in time.

Some of the oldest reaction patterns in our brains come from a time when the human race was living in the elements, without cars, restaurants and wi-fi. From an evolutionary perspective, some of those oldest reactions are:

- ○ Fight – to stay and fight an adversary

- ○ Flight – to head for the hills, probably because there is no way to beat the adversary

- ○ Freeze – to not move an inch because neither fighting nor flighting is going to work for us

Chances are, none of your customers live on the savannah and get chased by lions, tigers and bears on a daily basis. So, why is this relevant when you are selling?

It is relevant because these three responses are hardwired so deeply into our brains that they still get used on a daily basis. And they most definitely get used when we are buying something.

Understanding this part of our reaction pattern is especially important in order to know how we should present options to our customers.

One Option = Flight

Our brains are hardwired towards something known as 'single option aversion'. What that means in plain English is that if we are presented with only one option, our brains put up a big red flag to us and our instinctive reaction is to head for the hills.

That doesn't mean that you can't sell to someone if you only give them one option, but it does mean that you are making it a whole lot harder for yourself!

Two or Three Options = Fight

When we have two, or at the most three options, then our brains are happy. The headline talks about 'fight', but in this context it is not meant as something antagonistic. Instead, think of it as our customer both staying with us <u>and</u> engaging with us. In other words, behaving exactly how we want them to behave.

Another upshot of giving the customer more than one option is that the responsibility for the choice that is made lies clearly with your customer and not with you. If you only give your customer one option, then you have made the decision for them. It is on you whether that option turns out to be right for them or not.

If they arrive at the facility with their stuff and you have mis-judged how much space they need, then in the customer's mind it will naturally be your fault that the space doesn't fit. After all, you were the one who told them this is what they needed. By always making it the customer's choice, responsibility for that choice rests with your customer too. If there are hiccups or issues along the way, these will probably be written off as circumstance or bad luck instead of finger-pointing at you.

Four or More Options = Freeze

If we are presented with more than three options, then our brains are likely to wave another big red flag, but this one won't have us heading for the hills. This red flag in a sales situation will make our customers procrastinate.

Things will seem so complex that they will need more time to think it over and weigh different options against each other. In the meantime, they may very well end up renting storage from someone down the road who only gave them two options.

Heading Out to Sea

You have circled in on two or three options that you want to give your customer, so now the question is which one do you give them first?

Before I answer that question, I'd like to tell you about another handy little way that our brains work. When we are presented with something new, that we don't have a frame of reference for already, then we do what is called anchoring.

The way anchoring works is that the first thing we encounter becomes the anchor or the yardstick that we compare subsequent pieces of information against. It is also what we remember the best. What that means is that to our brains, it matters a whole lot which option we are given first in a selling situation!

The Intuitive Price Anchor

Most salespeople use anchoring in exactly the right way when they are giving prices to customers. It feels completely natural and intuitive to give the customer the smallest price first and that is exactly what we should be doing.

When we give the lowest price first, that is the price the customer will remember the best as they shop around for different options.

The Counter-Intuitive Space Anchor

So, what happens when a customer is at your facility and you are going to show them a few storage units? What a lot of people do is look at their vacant unit listing and find which unit is easy to get to or which units fit well to see together.

Put differently, it is often chance and location that decides which unit the customer sees first. If we do unit viewings like this, we are missing a trick in our sales process.

How many times have you shown a customer a storage unit and they have been surprised at how small a space you are suggesting to them? A lot of customers find it hard to imagine that their entire house can fit in to the unit you are showing them. In other words, a lot of customers already think the space we are suggesting feels small.

Using the principle of anchoring, if we show them the bigger unit first, then that will form the anchor or the yardstick for them to compare the second and smaller unit against.

Chances are, your customer will think the first and bigger unit feels small for all their stuff to fit in to. Then when you show them the smaller unit, it will probably feel too small to them and they will have a tendency to choose the bigger unit. And that leaves you with a higher value sale.

So, when you are showing customers around your facility, always show them the biggest unit first and then work your way down to the smaller options.

The Three-Sentence Rule

At this stage, you have given your customer the right number of options and presented them in the right order. Especially if your customer has never used self-storage before, you will also need to give them some general information about your facility.

If you have been able to unearth what your competition is, whether that is another storage operator or a friend's garage, you will also want to highlight why you are the better choice for them.

When you give your customers general information, the key is to keep it short. Always start off by giving top line information and then offer more detail if the customer asks for it.

Whether it is explaining the concept of self-storage or why your facility is the better choice, try setting yourself a three-sentence limit for this part of selling. Three sentences will fly by quicker than you might think, so this is something you can prepare beforehand and rehearse.

Extras

As we talked about in the last chapter on asking, any extra products or services you sell should be a natural part of any conversation you have about storage. I often see self-storage companies that treat storage and extras as two separate sales.

Unfortunately, this approach often cripples the turnover that extras can generate.

To really make the most of all the different offerings you have, treat your storage space and your extras as one big smorgasbord of solutions. Mix and match them depending on what your customer needs. Your customers will love you for it and so will your turnover.

Shopping Lists

While we are talking about extras, there is one trick that I see a lot of self-storage companies miss when they are selling, so we are going to cover it here.

When your customer has told you everything you need to know to estimate how much space they need, then you also know enough to estimate how many moving products they will need.

So why not finish off every storage enquiry by sending or giving the customer a shopping list of which moving products you think they will need?

You can make it nice and easy for them, with your logo, contact details and prices of your items. While you are at it, why not offer that if they want to have these products delivered straight to their door, you can arrange that for them too?

Just like customers rarely have a full understanding of how much space they will need, they also rarely have a full understanding of which moving products could save them time or protect their stuff.

Giving them a shopping list with your recommendations will set their expectation about what they will need. It also shows them you offer more than storage and that you know what you are talking about. A win on all accounts!

Get Your Environment to Sell for You

This final part of suggesting is less about how you explicitly present solutions to the customer. This is about how you can use the environment around you to support you in selling. Here are a few ideas to get your started:

o   Display testimonials in your reception area and around your facility.

o   Sell some of your smaller moving products in a vending machine, so that customers can buy them outside of your office hours.

o   Have information displays in your reception area, that visually show how some of your products can be used to either save money or protect belongings. Whenever you have more than one customer in your reception, the one waiting to be served will have something informative to look at.

o   Display moving boxes in a way so that it looks like the most natural way to buy them is in bundles of ten. If you offer free returns of unused boxes, most customers will be willing to take an extra pack of ten boxes, just in case.

o   Even for the smaller products, display as many of them as you can. By giving your customer a sense that you have volumes to sell, they will be more likely to buy volumes too.

These were just a few ideas, but there are many more. Let your creativity loose and take a walk through your facility to discover all the different ways it can help you sell more.

The Doggy Bag on Suggesting

- o Always present solutions as tailor-made to your customer, by linking what you suggest to what they have told you about their needs.

- o When it is time to give your customer general information about self-storage or about your company, keep it to three sentences or less.

- o The optimum amount of options to give a customer is two or three.

- o When giving the customer a price, give them the smallest price first.

- o When showing customers storage units, show them the biggest unit first.

- o Treat your sale of storage and your sale of extras (moving supplies, insurance etc.) as one sale instead of separate sales.

- o Finish off each sales conversation by giving your customer a shopping list over which moving products you think they will need.

- o Use your environment to help you sell.

Close

"The whole is greater than the sum of its parts."
Aristotle

Closing Time Happens All the Time

Welcome to the fourth step of the Spiral of Sales! By far the most important thing to realize about closing is that it doesn't just happen at the end of a sales process. When we sell, each step of the way contains some kind of close.

When a future customer visits our website, we might not be looking to close the storage space itself, although if you sell storage online then maybe that is your goal. A close on the website could just as well be to get the customer to make a reservation, to fill in a contact form or to open the live chat and speak to you online.

In the same way, when we are on the phone with someone, we might not be aiming to sell them the storage space right there and then. Our goal might be to get them to reserve a unit or to book them in for a site visit.

No matter how your sales process is pieced together, there will be different commitments that you want your customer to make at every step of your process. And each of those commitments are closes in their own right.

That is why the first step to really mastering the close is to be very clear about what you are closing at each step of your sales process. Are you closing a reservation? Are you closing a site visit? Are you closing a call-back in a few days?

As with many things in life and in business, things are easier and give us better results when we break them down into smaller steps. Closing works exactly like that.

In the chapter on trust, we talked about finishing off each step of the sales process by telling the customer what the next step is going to be. By doing this consistently, you are also doing yourself a big favor when it comes to the closing stage.

By consistently setting your customer's expectations, they will be prepared for what comes next. It lowers their resistance to the next step because they have time to prepare for it. This simple habit of always telling your customer what comes next can go a long way to increasing your close rate.

Relax! It's Just Closing Time!

Some people start feeling uncomfortable when the close approaches, because they feel awkward about asking for the sale. If you start feeling like this, you only have one task and that is to relax.

Relax, relax, relax!

Stay open and stay calm, because if you don't the customer will absolutely notice. And when they notice, they will tense up too. That leaves both of you feeling uncomfortable and reduces your chance of closing the sale. There simply are no winners in a scenario like that.

If you do feel nerves coming at any point, one of the quickest ways to calm yourself down is by making your exhale longer your inhale, when you breathe.

Breathing this way is the quickest way to tap into your own nervous system and trigger a relaxed response in your body. Your customer is unlikely to notice your breathing patterns, so add this to your pallet of techniques that you can use when needed. Your body and your sales numbers will thank you for it.

~~If~~ When

A great way to warm the customer up to signing the rental agreement is to speak to them in a way where we are assuming the sale. A very practical way to assume the sale is to replace 'if' with 'when' wherever it fits in to our conversations with the customer.

"~~If you choose to rent from us, then...~~"

"When you move in, then..."

Of course, this can be over-used. But wherever you can, speak to your customer in a way that just simply assumes that because they have contacted you about their storage needs, they will of course be moving in with you.

Ask for Permission

A soft and non-pushy way to open up to the close is to simply ask your customer for permission to do just that. Let me show you what I mean, by giving you a couple of examples:

"If you don't have any other questions then we are ready to move on to drawing up the rental contract. Is that okay with you?"

"The only thing left now is to run you through the rental contract. Is that okay with you?"

There are lots of different ways you can ask for permission. Whichever way comes naturally to you, you will find that closing becomes a much smoother process when you approach it this way.

By doing this you are not assuming that they are ready to buy, you are simply asking them if they are. If it turns out they are not, then they will be prompted to tell you why. Even if that is the case, your sales conversation will have gone one step further, even if you are not closing quite yet.

Know Your Birds

In the next chapter, we will start looking at the different customer types. Different customers like to be closed in different ways, so knowing your types is especially important then. Sometimes you will need to push a little for the close, while other times you will get further by giving the customer some space and time to think.

A Reason to Act

One way to give a customer that last little nudge to cross the finish line and sign that rental agreement is to give them a reason to act now. Giving them a reason why they shouldn't wait around.

You will recognize this from the world of retail, where pretty much any offer you come across is time limited. Giving customers a reason to act now may take the form of a discount that won't be available to them if they wait, but it doesn't have to.

Scarcity can be just as powerful a force to incentivize your customer to decide now rather than later.

"I don't have many units left in this size and I have had a lot of enquiries for this size category lately. So, if you want to make sure that it will be available when you need it, I would recommend reserving today."

If your customer is genuinely not ready to commit, maybe because they are a customer type that just needs more time to think, then this tactic won't have a big impact on them. But for customers who are ready, giving them a good reason why they should act now can be very helpful to getting that close.

The Power of Giving

A few chapters ago, we talked about likability being a big factor in who we choose to buy from. As it turns out, there is something even more powerful than likability. That something is reciprocity, or the power of giving.[ix]

Imagine that you are going into a shop to buy something and you have two choices:

1. Buy from a salesperson you don't really like, but they gave you something for free as you walked through the door.

2. Buy from a salesperson you do like, but they didn't give you anything as you walked through the door.

What research has shown[x] is that as consumers, we will consistently choose to buy from the first salesperson in this example.

Yes, you read that right!

We would rather buy from someone we don't like, if they have given us something with no strings attached. What happens is that when it comes to the time of closing the sale, we feel an urge to reciprocate and end up choosing them.

So, consider how you could incorporate this little 'brain hack' into your own sales process. What could you give away for free? It could be something as simple as giving your customer a cooled bottle of water, when they arrive at your site on a hot summer's day.

A hotel I stay at when I work in Italy has a little heating oven under the reception desk. Every time someone checks in, they open the oven and take out a warm chocolate chip cookie and hand to the guest.

Giving something away for free doesn't have to be expensive or complicated. But if you can find some way of giving without any strings attached, your customer is much more likely to choose you over the competition when it is time to sign the rental agreement.

Haragei: The Art of the Stomach

If you are twisting your tongue trying to pronounce the headline of this section, don't worry. It translates easily into the English saying that silence is golden.

Translated literally from Japanese, 'haragei' means 'the art of the stomach'. It describes the silence that is common practice to have in Japanese business dealings.

Whereas a Western business meeting will unlikely have more than a few seconds of silence before someone jumps in and says something, silence is used frequently in Japan. It isn't unusual to have up to 40 seconds of prolonged silence and this is often seen as the most productive part of the meeting.

As you will soon learn in the section on different customer types, different customers will need varying amounts of time and silence to decide whether they want to buy from you or not.

As a salesperson, the important thing to know is that this silence is quite literally golden. Brian Tracey, who is one of the biggest authorities on sales in the world, says this about silence: "The sale takes place with the words, but the buying takes place in the silence".[xi]

So, if things get quiet, try to resist the temptation to jump in and break the silence. If it nerves you, try counting to five or ten inside your head and let your customer be the one to break the silence.

The Only Rule That Matters in Negotiating

In some situations, you might end up in a negotiation with your customer. There are heaps of books written about how to negotiate successfully, but as you might have noticed I am a big fan of keeping things simple. Negotiating is no exception.

When you negotiate with a customer, there is actually only one rule of thumb that matters:

Always negotiate on a different parameter than your customer.

What that means is that if your customer wants you to lower your price, then you make sure to stay away from negotiating on price.

If you don't, then the negotiation will end up having a winner and a loser; one of you will get their way and the other one won't. So, either your customer walks away feeling like they lost that one, or you walk away having compromised the value of your sale. Neither of those scenarios benefit you in any way.

By always negotiating on a different parameter to your customer, you can avoid this scenario all together. You can reach an agreement where both of you walk away as winners.

If your customer wants to negotiate on price, then you could negotiate on unit size, unit location or upfront payment, just to mention a few examples. This is what it could sound like:

"If the price is too high for you, then I can offer you a unit on the 1st floor at the back of the building. It is the same size, but just take a little longer to get to."

"If the price is too high, then I can drop it by 10% if you can prepay the first year of rent."

"If the price is too high then we could move you down one unit size. It would be a bit of a squeeze, but if you want to save on the monthly rent then that would be an option."

When you take this approach to negotiating, your customer is going to respond in one of two ways.

If the thing they are negotiating on is a sincere concern of theirs (for example, they just can't afford it), then they will accept one of your other suggestions.

But if they are negotiating with you just to see if they can get a discount, then this approach will show them in a very soft and pleasant way that you are not going to budge on price. If this is the case, the customer will probably agree with the price you offered to start with, and the negotiation will be over.

Either way, you both walk away as winners.

The Doggy Bag on Closing

- Closing doesn't just happen once at the end of a sale. It happens at every stage of your process, so be clear about what you are closing at each stage.

- Relax, stay calm and stay open when you are closing.

- Replace 'if' with 'when' to assume the sale in your sales conversations.

- To softly ease in to the close, ask your customer for permission to close them.

- Adapt your closing style to the customer type you are dealing with.

- Giving something away for free with no strings attached will help you close sales.

- Find a way to be comfortable with a bit of silence in the closing situation.

- If you end up in a negotiation, always negotiate on a different parameter than your customer.

The Four Customer Types

"Share our similarities, celebrate our differences."
M. Scott Peck

Does One Size Fit All?

Think for a moment about the people closest to you; a spouse, partner or friend. If you are in a shop with them, how do they like to buy things? Are they very similar to you or do they go about it differently?

You can probably think of one or more people close to you that go about buying things very differently to you. Maybe they like to take their time, whereas you want to get it over with. Maybe you like to chat to the salesperson, whereas they want to chat as little as possible.

This is exactly why we need to understand and adapt to the type of customer we are dealing, if we want to get our conversion rate as high as possible. One size doesn't fit all; it is not true for clothing and it is definitely not true for sales.

Most salespeople already adapt intuitively to their customer to some extent, but it can be difficult to know exactly what our customer needs if they are very different to us. That is why having a model and a framework is helpful. It helps us classify and adapt, so that we can get even better at tailoring our approach to the customer we are dealing with.

The model on customer types that we are going to be looking closer at is based on a behavioral profiling system known as DISC[xii]. This system is often used for recruitment and team development, and sometimes for sales too.

I have translated this system into something that is quick to learn and easy to remember. Each customer type is presented as a bird, that we all know and can relate to.

The Ornithology of Sales

In the grid on the next page, you will notice that there are two axes.

The horizontal axis has task-focused types on the left-hand side and people-focused types on the right-hand side.

The vertical axis has the louder, outgoing types at the top and the quieter, more reserved types at the bottom.

In each quadrant you find one customer type:

Eagles: these are louder types who are very task focused.

Parrots: these are outgoing types who are very people oriented.

Doves: these are quieter types who are very people oriented.

Owls: these are reserved types who are very task focused.

In the following chapters you will learn some quick ways to spot which type you are dealing with, even if all you have from them is an email. After that, we take a look at how you can adapt your approach to each of these types and most importantly how to close the sale with them.

As you learn about each of these types, you will notice that they are described as stereotypes or extremes. In reality, very few people have behavior that is as clear-cut as you will read in the following chapters.

The Four Customer Types

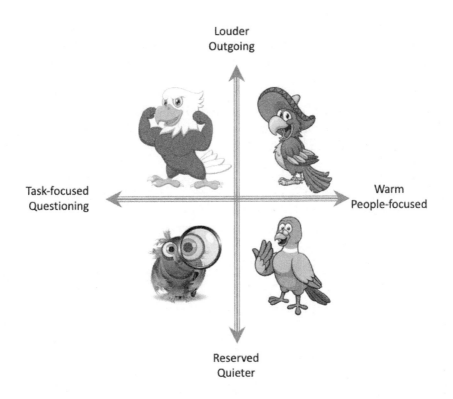

That is because we all have a little bit of each of these four birds within us. Which trait comes out the strongest depends on the situation we are in and how stressed we are.

Even though our personalities are far more complex than a simple four quadrant grid, there are fundamentally four different behaviors that dominate when we are in a buying situation.

As you go through the next chapters, try to identify which type you are when you are selling, and which type you are when you are buying. For many people they are the same, but they don't have to be.

Building self-awareness about your own communication style will help you become aware of how you need to adapt when you are dealing with customers that are very different to you.

Selling to Eagles

"He does not always choose the best Who muses long."
Johann Wolfgang von Goethe

Eagle = Powerful

If we were to sum up the eagle customer in only one word, that word would be 'powerful'. Eagles are the natural born leaders of our world and you won't be surprised to hear that many eagles find themselves in high ranking positions in their professional lives.

Eagles are direct, assertive, decisive and competitive! And whether they are selling or buying, their style is very telling. They will take charge of the conversation and they will tell you what they need and what they want.

Eagles are a louder, out-going type who are very task-oriented. When they get in touch with you, their perspective is that they have a problem that needs solving and they want this to happen in the quickest and most efficient way. They won't want to waste any time with small talk and will get straight to the point.

These are people who are always on the go and always multitasking, so you will need to move fast to keep their interest up. If you are speaking to an eagle on the phone you can be sure that they are doing at least two or three other things while they speak to you. So, you will need to grab their attention and keep it!

Long-winded details, repetitive conversations and things moving along slowly are the types of things that eagles get agitated by.

How to Spot an Eagle

Because eagles are task-focused, they will be very matter of fact in the way they present their question or need to you. They will be direct, blunt and brief in their style and if they are writing to you, you might not even get a greeting! They won't give you a lot of personal information or tell you stories about why they need storage. They will approach this as a task that needs to be solved:

They need storage.

You offer storage.

You can probably fix their problem.

End of story.

Eagles tend to have a strong handshake and when you meet them, they will probably lean forward and look you straight in the eye. They are generally strong in their eye contact throughout a conversation and they will expect you to be too.

These are action-oriented people who want to get stuff done, so they might be more comfortable standing up than sitting down if they come for a site visit. Even if they agree to sit down, these are energetic and fast-paced people, so they won't lean back and sit still. They will more likely lean forward and want to hurry up.

Eagles tend to have a more contained body posture, but they will use lots of hand gestures when they speak.

They also care a lot about how they present themselves to the world and they like to dress in a way that shows you just how successful they are. They are likely to be wearing expensive clothes, but you are unlikely to find them in the latest fashion. They tend to prefer classic style clothes that are beautifully made.

An eagle will want to control the conversation with you and since they don't like detail, they will probably interrupt you if you get too detailed with them.

What an email from an eagle could look like:

Melissa.

Appointment in the diary. Need to know if I should bring anything.

Steven

(I'm not kidding, that's all they would write.)

How Others See Eagles

While eagles see themselves as the straight talking, action-oriented natural leader, you might feel differently about eagles if you have a different type to them.

If you are a parrot yourself, you might think that they are being unfriendly, because they are not as chatty and storytelling as you are.

If you are a dove, you might feel like eagles are being impatient and insensitive, because of their brief and blunt style.

If you are an owl, you might think that eagles are a bit sloppy because they skip too many details. From the owl's perspective, if eagles would just slow down and take the time for the finer detail, they would be able to take in the whole picture before making a decision and be better off for it.

Selling to an Eagle

When you are selling to an eagle, be prepared to be challenged! Even though eagles love control and feel at the their best when they are the one in charge, you will gain their respect if you stand up to them in an unemotional and matter-of-fact kind of way.

If things move slowly or get too detailed the eagle will get impatient, so especially if you are more of a dove or owl yourself, you will need to speed up in order to match the pace of the eagle. Skip the small talk, get to the point quickly and give them top line information only. Throughout the sales process, keep an eye out for signs of impatience from the eagle. If you don't notice any, you are on the right track with them.

Eagles are multi-taskers! Since they always have a lot going on, they are also unlikely to be planning far ahead in the future. That means that when they contact you, their need is likely to be very soon or right now.

Behavior	Likes	Dislikes
Brief	Efficiency	Too much detail
Blunt	Getting stuff done	Repetitive conversations
Direct	Being in control	Wasting time
Assertive	Challenges	Small talk
Decisive	A quick pace	
Competitive	Top line information	
Interrupts	Classic appearance	
Firm handshake		
Strong eye contact		

Closing an Eagle

Eagles like to be in charge. They love the feeling of making decisions, getting stuff done and being in control. So, when you get to the closing stage with an eagle it is important that you let them be the one to make the decision. Especially for this customer type, it will be more important than ever to give them several options and let them make the final choice.

When you are closing an eagle, just be as direct with them as they are with you:

"Based on what we have just covered, should I draw up the rental contract for you to sign?"

Because they are both decisive and likely to have a need very soon, you should be leaving an interaction with an eagle with some kind of commitment from them.

P.S.

You will notice that this book has a 'doggy bag' at the end of each chapter. Since eagles like top line information, that summary has been added especially for the eagle readers of this book.

The Doggy Bag on Eagles

- o   Watch for signs of impatience.

- o   Be direct and straight-talking.

- o   Stick to top-line information and avoid detail unless the eagle asks for it.

- o   Emails from an eagle will be brief and may not even contain a greeting.

- o   Their need is likely to be soon or right now.

- o   If you are a dove or an owl yourself, speed up when you are dealing with an eagle.

Selling to Parrots

"Those who tell the stories rule the world."
Hopi American Indian proverb

Parrot = Popular

The one-word description of the parrot customer would be 'popular'. Parrots are talkative, social types who love to interact with others. They love human connection and they love to tell stories. If you met a parrot in an elevator, they would be the type that strikes up a conversation with you straight away. They might even hold the door open when they get to their floor, so they can finish the story they are telling. So, it might not surprise you to hear that a lot of parrots end up in people-focused professional roles. There are actually a fair amount of them in the field of sales.

Whether they work in sales or not, their style is very 'selling' in that classic sense of the word. Talkative, persuasive, enthusiastic, charismatic and magnetic!

Parrots are often creative people who like something innovative and new. To them, change is fun! They like new experiences and they place a very high value on freedom and flexibility. The flipside of that is that routine, processes and sticking to rules are a real bore to the parrot.

Because they are such outgoing and people-loving types, social recognition is very important to them. They care what other people think and they don't want to lose popularity or image by the choices they make. The parrot customer will also care just as much about who they are buying from as what they are buying, so they will want to get to know you a little.

How to Spot a Parrot

When you encounter a parrot, you will first of all notice that they are talkative, energetic and fast-paced. They will use colorful, exaggerated language. These are the customers who will use words like 'awesome' and 'fantastic'.

A parrot might jump from one thing to the next when they speak, and they might even interrupt you as something pops into their mind while you are talking.

You will notice that their facial expressions and hand gestures are dynamic and active when they speak. They might not settle for just hand gestures but move their whole body around, as they tell you the story of why they are speaking to you today.

Parrots like to be seen; they thrive on attention. As a result, you are likely to find them dressed in the latest fashion and if you see a customer wearing bright colors, they are probably a parrot.

How Others See Parrots

Parrots see themselves as dynamic and engaging people, who can bring motivation, enthusiasm and smiles to the people around them. If you are not a parrot yourself, they might come across differently to you though.

If you are an eagle, then you might find the parrots to be too over-the-top and too friendly. You might feel like they are wasting time with all their talking and socializing and should focus more on just getting stuff done.

If you are a dove, you might feel like the parrots are too talkative and if a parrot talks too much without inviting you into the conversation, they could come across as insensitive and a bit self-centered to you.

What an email from a parrot could look like:

Hey Melissa yup thursday works for me....I'm excited to see your site!! If I'm a little late on Thursday then don't worry I'll be on my way! I'm coming straight from the hair dresser and that guy just loves to talk...

By the way the moving company called me after we hung up earlier and said that they aren't available that day after all they have double booked themselves apparently!! So I need to find another one...do you know of anyone good?

See you Thursday, Steve

(They love exclamation marks!!! And don't get me started on their punctuation, spelling and grammar...)

If you are an owl, then you have very little in common with the parrot! You could feel like they are unrealistically optimistic in their approach to most things. You might think that the way they can exaggerate their language takes away from the accuracy of what they are saying.

Selling to a Parrot

Parrots will tell you stories while you sell to them, so let them talk and be prepared to listen! Then gently steer the conversation in the direction you want it to be going. Because of their love for storytelling and talking, they tend to not be the best listeners in the world though.

So, keep details to a minimum when you speak to them and agree that you will email all the details they need. That way, the parrot can reference the details when they need them, and you avoid any misunderstandings about it.

Parrots love things that are new, different and popular so tell your parrot customer how you stand out from the crowd; what makes you different than the rest. If you have any big, famous companies that rent from you then mention those too. Parrots care what other people think, which means testimonials make an even bigger impact on these customers. So, display them where you can, both online and around your reception or site.

Parrots care about who they are buying from so show them the person behind the name. Be prepared to share a personal story or two if you really want to bond with a parrot.

If you are a dove or an owl, you will need to speed up when you are dealing with parrots. Their natural pace is higher than yours, so ramp things up to match the parrot, so you keep them engaged and interested.

Behavior	Likes	Dislikes
Outgoing	Creativity	Routine
Talkative	Choice	Processes
Enthusiastic	Freedom	Sticking to rules
Informal	Social recognition	Detail
Personal	Innovation	
Lots of gestures	Change	
Exaggerated language	Trendy clothes	
	Bright colors	
	Attention	

Closing a Parrot

Parrots like flexibility, freedom and choice, so just like the eagles it with be very important to give them options and let them be the ones to make the decision.

When you are approaching the close with a parrot, keep it informal, relaxed and conversational. You could say something like:

"This sounds like the right place for you, how about I start up the paperwork for this while we keep chatting?"

Just like eagles, parrots are likely to have a need very soon and they are not afraid of making a choice straight away. That is why it is important that you finish off your interaction with a parrot with some kind of commitment.

The Doggy Bag on Parrots

- o Be personal, conversational and informal.

- o Confirm details in an email rather than building it in to conversation; the parrot won't remember it if you just tell them.

- o They like things that are new, creative and different, so tell the parrot how your site stands out from the crowd.

- o They care about what other people think, so make the most of any testimonials or references you have.

- o Their need is likely to be soon or right now, so you can close them on the day.

- o If you are a dove or an owl yourself, speed up when you are dealing with parrot customers.

Selling to Doves

"If you wish to experience peace, provide peace for another."
Dalai Lama

Dove = Peaceful

If you describe an encounter with a dove in only one word, that word would probably be 'peaceful'. They are reserved, but people-oriented and come across as sincere and warm.

Doves care a lot about other people and they often put the need of others ahead of their own. It even shows in their language; they are much more likely to say 'we' and 'us' instead of 'me' and 'I'.

These are patient and loyal people, who thrive in an environment that is harmonious and cooperative. They like stability and maintaining the status quo, so as I'm sure you can imagine they are not the biggest embracers of change.

To a dove, change means uncertainty and instability and they don't feel comfortable with it at all. That is reflected in their decision making, which tends to be slower than that of the eagle and the parrot.

Their love for harmony goes so far that if they disagree with you, they are actually unlikely to tell you. In fact, doves hide their emotions more often than not.

They are very good listeners and will come across as under-stated and understanding.

How to Spot a Dove

Doves are the most difficult type to spot, so if you are ever in doubt about which customer type you are dealing with, chances are it is a dove.

They are soft-spoken and with a friendly and conversational style. Doves listen more than they speak, especially in the beginning. They also have an agreeable, respectful and sensitive style towards others.

Their body language is open and relaxed, but they won't use many hand gestures when they speak. The ones they do make will be calmer and slower than what you will get from the parrot, for instance.

Their eye contact can be a bit unstable when they speak to you. They might look at the floor, the ceiling or to the side as they speak to you.

Doves put substance over style, and they put comfort over style too. That is why you are unlikely to find them in expensive clothes and extravagant fashion. You are much more likely to find them wearing comfortable clothes that are more neutral in style.

How Others See Doves

Doves see themselves as steady, balanced and loyal people who are kind and caring towards others. But if you are not a dove yourself, you might see them differently.

If you are an eagle, you might feel like the dove is too slow in making decisions and that they resist change too much. They are 'wordier' than you and you wish they would just get to the point!

If you are a parrot, you might think that the dove is too quiet, modest and careful. If they just let go a little they could have so much more fun!

What an email from a dove could look like:

Hi Melissa,

Thanks for sending through the confirmation, I really appreciate it. I am looking forward to seeing your facility and talking through the different options on Thursday.

You mentioned that you also cooperate with a moving company. If you could forward their details to me, that would be really helpful. Moving is such a big deal anyway, this might be able to make it all a little smoother.

Thanks again and kind regards,

Steven

(They take a little longer to get to the point, but see how pleasant and soft-spoken they are?)

If you are an owl, you might think that the dove wastes too much time caring for other people and that they should spend that time on the details of the matter instead.

Selling to a Dove

The most important thing when you are selling to doves is to fully acknowledge that change is difficult for them. In that sense, it is likely that every single dove customer you deal with will be outside their comfort zone. That is because when people need storage space, it is usually because they are going through some kind of change. They are relocating, getting married, getting divorced, starting a business, expanding a business or moving home.

The reasons can be many, but most of our customers find themselves in some kind of change when they contact us. The eagle will see that change as a task to be conquered. The parrot will see it as a fun and exciting challenge. To the dove, it is just uncomfortable, hard work that brings uncertainty and instability with it.

That means that most doves you encounter when you are selling self-storage will be stressed. But because they are masters at hiding their emotions, they probably won't show you just how stressed they are. Any reassurances and relief you can offer that will take stress away from them will go a long way towards making you stand out from their other storage options.

Doves are fundamentally people-oriented and combined with their other traits it means that they want you to show a sincere interest in them as people. They want to know that you sincerely care.

Listen carefully to what they tell you, don't interrupt or be abrupt with them. They will have chosen their words carefully and whatever they do tell you will mean something to them; doves rarely talk just for the sake of talking.

Behavior	Likes	Dislikes
Calm	Harmony	Change
Steady	Cooperation	Pressure
Patient	Stability	Stress
Loyal	The status quo	Conflict
Caring	Helping others	
Puts others first	Feeling part of something bigger	
Listens more than they speak	Comfortable clothes	
Hides their emotions		
Under-stated		

Because doves like reliability and stability, anything you can do to show that you are a dependable choice will help you make a good impression. Whether it is a guarantee, testimonials, awards or certificates, they all help in showing the dove that you are someone they can count on.

If your company does any charity work, the dove is the one you want to make sure to tell! They like helping others and feeling part of something bigger than themselves, so tell them about any charities you support or who rent from you.

Closing a Dove

The single most important part of closing a dove is to never, ever leave them feeling like you are pressuring them in to buying from you.

If they feel like that is what you are doing, they will mentally be heading straight for the door. But they will be too polite and friendly to tell you that you have just overstepped your boundaries with them. So, the key to successfully closing a sale with a dove is to give them the space and the time they need to make their decision.

This also means that if you are an eagle or a parrot yourself, then you will need to slow down when you are dealing with a dove. Your natural pace will be higher than theirs. So, in order to not give them the impression that you are hurrying them along, you will need to take a breath and go a bit slower.

If they say they want to think it over, it probably doesn't mean that they are stalling or making excuses. There is a decent chance they actually want to think it through. If that is the case, agree a date and a time when you will call them back to follow up. Make sure you set their expectations about the decision needing to be made then, so they are ready for it.

Because doves are deductive and slower decision makers and they can be reluctant towards change, they are unlikely to commit straight away. That is why you will find that a dove goes through your sales process quicker if you always prepare them for what the next step is going to be. With that preparation time, it will mean they have less resistance to that step once it arrives.

On a very practical level, it helps to refer to following a process when you are closing a dove. It could go something like this:

"Now that we have found the size and specific unit you need, the next step is to draw up the rental contract so I can talk you through that step of the process. Is that ok with you?"

Doves are loyal types, so these are the customers that will stick with you through thick and thin once they decide that you are worthy of their trust.

The dove is the customer type who is most likely to refer you to their friends and family, even if you don't ask them to. A parrot would also happily refer if they got something in return, but the dove will do it unprompted if they like their experience with you.

The Doggy Bag on Doves

- o Doves will be the most stressed by change when they speak to you, but because they hide their emotions well, they may not seem stressed.

- o Avoid applying pressure when you sell to them. If they are not ready to buy, agree a follow-up with them instead of insisting on a close.

- o Explain why you are a reliable and secure choice.

- o Highlight any charity work that your company does.

- o Doves are likely to dress in comfortable clothes with a more neutral style.

- o If you are an eagle or a parrot yourself, slow your pace down when dealing with a dove.

- o Refer to a process when you are closing a dove.

- o If a dove says "I want to think about it", it probably means they want to actually think about it (not just stall the decision).

Selling to Owls

"The Devil is in the details, but so is salvation."
Hyman G. Rickover

Owls = Perfect

If we sum up owls in only one word, it would of course be 'perfect'. They are detail-loving people who are natural born planners! So, it may not surprise you to hear that a lot of owls end up in jobs that relate to engineering, accounting and law.

The owl's detailed nature has two main consequences.

First of all, they are very cautious people. If you are aware of all the detail that can go wrong, then it makes sense that you would be more cautious, right?

Second of all, it means they value quality very highly. They notice if your website and your brochure give conflicting information, or whether there is a fine layer of dust on top of your moving boxes in your reception. They truly value quality when they see it. To them, quality means consistency with a strong attention to detail.

Owls like accuracy and efficiency, but they would rather do something right than do it quickly. Their standards are high, as are their expectations of other people. They love facts and logic and their approach is very methodical.

The flipside of this is of course that owls don't like it when they notice things that are disorganized or sloppy. They expect you to be knowledgeable and give them the facts. That is why they will quickly lose interest if they notice you being careless with details or if there are too many questions you can't answer.

Because they are cautious people, who plan ahead and take their time, you will need to buckle in for the long haul when you are selling to an owl. It won't be a quick process, but when you close them, they will be completely sure that you are the best choice for them.

How to Spot an Owl

Owls are task-focused and reserved, so they won't share much personal information with you when they first enquire. They will treat it as a task that needs to be solved and might even seem a bit cold or formal at first. Owls might only shake your hand very briefly and they are likely to cross their arms when they speak to you.

Their body language will be a bit more closed and they won't use a lot of hand gestures when they speak. If they do, the movements will be more contained. Their facial expressions will be more neutral, and their style will be direct, but also calm and measured at the same time.

Maybe the easiest way to spot an owl is by all the questions they will ask you! The owl will want to understand every detail of what you offer before deciding if you are the one they choose.

Owls will usually look formal and smart in their clothing choices. The way they present themselves will be immaculate, but you probably won't find them wearing the expensive brands that the eagle likes. After weighing up the quality and price, the owl's wardrobe will be a measured balancing act between the two.

What an email from an owl could look like:

Hi Melissa,

Thanks for sending through the confirmation for my site visit on Thursday at 10 am. After our conversation earlier, I reviewed your website again and ask that you send me more information about the following before my visit:

1. Are heated units available only on the ground floor or also on upper levels?

2. How much notice do you require of me when I move out of storage?

3. Does the deposit payment only refer to rent or to insurance as well?

4. Is the access code to the property gate and the building gate the same or different to each other?

Yours Sincerely,

Steven

(Yeah, buckle in for the long haul when you are selling to owls.)

How Others See Owls

Owls see themselves as the methodical and reasonable one in the crowd. They collect all the information, review it and then make the best choice. Is there any other way to make good decisions? If you are not an owl yourself, you might feel differently about this approach and you might see them differently as a result.

If you are an eagle, you might think that the owl pays way too much attention to insignificant details and that they could get so much more done if they just focused on the top-line information.

If you are a parrot, you might feel like they are too conservative and pessimistic in their approach and that they should have a bit more faith in the brighter side of life.

If you are a dove, you might feel like the owl is too cold and doesn't care enough about other people.

Selling to an Owl

The most important thing to know about selling to owls is that because they are methodical and precise, they will do their research. They will compare your offer with every single competing option under the sun! But owls are also reserved, so they are probably not going to tell you just how much shopping around they are doing.

That means that especially with owls, it is vital that you tell them all the ways in which you are different to the competition and why you are the better choice for them.

When an owl buys something, they want to know that they are doing things right and that they have factored every eventuality in to their decision. So have brochures or other materials to hand that you can give them to take away and study.

Owls are task-oriented and often prefer to keep things formal, so only ask them personal questions if they initiate it first.

Behavior	Likes	Dislikes
Precise	Detail	Sloppiness
Questioning	Accuracy	Carelessness
Formal in tone	High standards	Being disorganized
Cautious	Logic	Being in a rush
Crossed arms when they speak to you	Planning ahead	Inconsistency
May go silent in a conversation	Quality	Feeling pressured
Neutral in their handshake and facial expressions	Being methodical	
	Privacy	
	Peace and quiet	

Be specific and precise when you speak to them and do exactly what you have told them you are going to do. If you don't, they will most definitely notice!

Owls take in a lot of detail and sometimes that means they need to think things through on the spot before they respond to you. So, when you are dealing with an owl, you will need to be comfortable with a bit of silence once in a while. This can feel tricky, especially if you are an eagle or a parrot yourself.

If you are an eagle or a parrot, you will also need to slow down when you are dealing with an owl, in order to not make them feel like you are rushing them.

Closing an Owl

Just like doves, owls will take their time making a buying decision and you need to give them that time to successfully close them. They are unlikely to make a commitment straight away, so if you can't close them on your first interaction, agree a follow-up and the next steps instead.

Be careful not to push too hard for the close, because although they won't react as strongly as the dove does, it will definitely reduce your chances with them.

When an owl says 'I'll think about it', they are similar to the doves. It probably doesn't mean they are trying to stall or make excuses; they just genuinely want more time to think things over. Owls like to plan ahead, which means their need is likely to be further into the future. So, the way they see it, they have plenty of time to think.

When you are closing an owl, you can use their affinity to process and detail to your advantage by referring to it in your close:

"Now that we have covered all the detail of what we offer, how about we go through the rental agreement point by point, so you also have a full understanding of the contract?"

If an owl is on the fence about whether or not to choose you, then give them as objective advice as possible. This would be a perfect time to practice a bit of that un-selling we talked about a few chapters ago!

Give them the pros and a few cons about renting from you, but of course be selective in which cons you present them with, so that you still help yourself in the close.

The Doggy Bag on Owls

- o The owl will ask you a lot of questions!

- o They are detail-oriented, precise and like to plan ahead.

- o They are the customer type who is most likely to shop around with your competitors, so tell them what makes you stand out from the crowd.

- o Give owls time to think and if you can't close them straight away, agree a call-back.

- o Only ask personal questions if the owl initiates it.

- o Owls are cautious and value high quality.

- o If you are an eagle or a parrot yourself, you need to slow down when you are dealing with an owl.

Objections

"Different roads sometimes lead to the same castle."
George R. R. Martin

Friend or Foe?

Many sales books and sales courses claim that when we get objections in sales, it is a buying signal. It is a sign that our customer is getting ready to buy. The logic here is that objections should be welcomed and celebrated, not feared.

In some ways they are right. One of the biggest obstacles to making a sale is indifference; when our customer fundamentally couldn't care less who they buy from. When a customer objects they are showing enough interest in our offering to object to buying it, so at least there is no indifference there.

But with that said, if it was really true that objections should be celebrated as a buying signal from our customers, then the more experienced a salesperson gets, the more objections they would trigger in their customers. The thing is, anyone with practical experience in sales will probably have noticed that the opposite tends to be true.

Prevention Is the Best Medicine

Experienced salespeople tend to get less objections than sales newbies, because the more experienced we get the better we are at preventing objections from coming up in the first place.

We learn how to pace the conversation and ask the right questions. We show the customer that we are the expert and sometimes we might even challenge our customer's thinking about self-storage.

We learn how to show them that there is a different way to do things that will save them space or make their move more efficient. We manage the customer's expectations throughout the sales process and tell them what is coming next, so that when it is time for the next step, the customer is ready and less likely to object.

Although this chapter is mainly about how we handle objections once they do pop up, the goal when we sell should always be to improve our objection prevention. Not only will that reduce the number of objections that come our way, it will also tend to make the objections we get more genuine.

Sometimes customers object just because they don't feel ready to buy. They feel like they need more time before they decide. As our sales skills improve over time, we get better at preparing our customers. When we do that, the 'I'm just not ready' type objections go away. The ones that are left are the ones that are genuine, true objections. Those are the ones we really want to be dealing with and handling.

Objection handling is when sales really and truly becomes a skill! Until the first objection arrives, the role of a salesperson can be more like an information giver or an order taker.

When objections are added to the mix, that is when salespeople really get to show what they are made of. As your experience grows, you will find that you don't just handle objections better. You prevent them from arising altogether.

What's Behind the Scenes?

Another important point around objection handling is to be clear on what an objection actually means. Yes, the customer is saying 'no' to what we have just offered to sell them, but <u>why</u> are they saying no? It can seem like an obvious question, but it is less obvious when we take a closer look.

Let's take the example of a customer telling you they think your quote is too expensive. What could be the underlying reason why someone thinks it is too expensive?

Here is a list of 13 reasons, but I am sure there are more:

1. Feels like they are not getting value for money.

2. Wants something for nothing and no offer will ever be low enough.

3. Doesn't know what the price really involves.

4. Genuinely can't afford it.

5. Can get the same space cheaper from another self-storage operator.

6. Hasn't made any comparisons yet.

7. Is out for a discount.

8. Wants to know more before they decide.

9. Doesn't feel ready to buy and price was the first thing that came to their mind.

10. Has a fixed price in their mind and what you have offered is different to that.

11. Received a previous quote that was cheaper, so the price you have offered is different than they expected.

12. Had a bad customer service experience with your company at some point during the sales process.

13. Provoking you to test your reaction.

Depending on what the underlying reason for the objection is, it will need to be handled differently. That is the reason why all objection handling has to be adapted to the unique circumstances of your customer. There isn't one way of doing objection handling; there are as many ways as there are customers.

What is both important and helpful though, is to have a framework for ourselves that helps us include all the necessary components of good objection handling into these unique circumstances. That is what we are going to take a look at now.

The Circle Becomes A Spiral

When we get an objection, that is the moment that the circle of sales turns in to the Spiral of Sales. The process that we go through when we handle an objection is the same as when we start a sale from scratch. When we get a 'no' from a customer, no matter what form that 'no' takes, we take one more loop in the circle, but we make that circle smaller and smaller until we reach the final close.

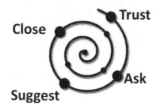

Confirm Trust

This is the first step after we get an objection and it is by far the most important one. That is because until now in the sales process, you and the customer have been on the same side, figuratively speaking.

They have been sharing information with you and you have been finding solutions for them. After the first close doesn't succeed, the most important thing is to quickly reaffirm to the customer that you are <u>still</u> on the same side.

The way we do that is to tell the customer that it is okay that they just objected. We can do that without agreeing with the objection itself. It could sound something like this:

"That's a great question, thank you for bringing that up."

"I understand your hesitation, I should have been clearer when I told you about that earlier."

~~But~~ And

On a very practical level, one way of subtly confirming trust is to replace 'but' with 'and' when we speak to our customer. Try taking a look at these two identical sentences and see what a difference it makes whether we use 'but' or 'and'.

*"I understand why that's a concern **and** I'd like to tell you a bit more about that part of our setup, so you have the full picture."*

Now compare that to:

*"I understand why that's a concern **but** I'd like to tell you a bit more about that part of our setup, so you have the full picture."*

If you read those two sentences out loud to yourself, you will probably notice that when you use 'but', it sounds like you are more on the defense. It sounds like you are objecting to their objection.

When you use 'and' instead, you sound accepting of their point of view and are continuing the conversation based on what the customer just told you.

Clarifying Questions

If you are in any way in doubt about what the customer means by their objection or why they are objecting, then this is the time to ask them clarifying questions. Once you are clear on what exactly their objection is, it is also important to ask the customer if they have any other concerns or objections.

The reason we do that is twofold.

First of all, if the customer has any more objections then it is important to unearth what they are before we try to close again.

And second of all, if the customer says they don't have any other objections, then that is your opening to start closing them again.

Suggesting Perspective

In the suggestion phase of objection handling it is all about giving your customer another perspective on their objection. Show them that although you understand why they see things in a certain way, you would like to offer another perspective on the topic that could help them in their decision making.

The Next Close

Finally, it is time to try closing them again. When we close the second, third or fourth time it is important that we user softer, not harder, language to ease in to the close. That is how we signal that things are still relaxed, friendly and non-pushy. You could use phrases like:

"Moving forward"

"Take the next step"

"Do the paperwork"

"Show the contract"

A Practice Run

So, let's take all those parts of the Spiral of Sales and put them together in to one response. Imagine your customer has just told you that they think your quote is too expensive. Your response could go something like this:

"I understand why price is a concern, moving can be both stressful and expensive. If I was in your position, I would also want to make sure that I was getting the best deal. It can be a bit confusing to compare different options, because not everyone lists their prices in the same way.

Whenever I have customers who compare our site with other options, they usually come to the conclusion that we end up as the cheapest option, once they have factored in all the costs.

Storing with the moving company you mentioned earlier for example, means that you would be charged a fee every time you want to access your stuff, whereas here by us you have unlimited access for your fixed monthly rent.

So, between that and our price guarantee that I told you about earlier, I do think that this is a really competitive price for the space you will need.

Do you have any other concerns about renting from us, or was price the only one?"

If the customer doesn't have other concerns, we could then close again by saying:

"Okay, in that case are you ready for me to show you the contract?"

This is how we go around the Spiral of Sales until we either reach a point where we close the customer, or we have a definitive 'no' to our offer.

What Is Your Fallback Sale?

If you do get a definitive 'no', then you need a plan for what to do. The person you have been speaking to doesn't want to buy from you now, but they might want to come back in the future. They might know people who they would be willing to recommend you to. Their first choice for storage might fall through and they could find their way back to you. It takes both effort and money to get enquiries into a business, so even if customers say 'no' we should still be getting as much value from every enquiry that comes our way.

One way of doing that is to have a pre-defined fallback sale in place. A fallback sale is what you sell the customer if they don't want to buy what you are trying to sell. A fallback sale doesn't need to be financial in any kind of way. It could be a callback later that week. It could be a non-binding reservation. It could be a sign-up to your quarterly newsletter to people in the area.

Whatever it is, be clear on what your fallback sale is so that when you get that definitive 'no', you can jump straight into closing your fallback, instead of the one you were hoping to close.

The Greatest Hits

There are four main objections that I have seen transcend individual markets and companies. We are now going to take a closer look at how we can handle these in the best way.

"I Need to Think About It"

If your customer is a dove or an owl, then they might genuinely need to think it over before they decide whether to rent from you. So, if you do get this objection, try closing them one more time. If that doesn't work, agree a date and time where you can call them back to follow up, instead of pushing for yet another close. For example:

"I understand you want to think this through, so you are sure you are making the right choice. The thing is, I don't have many units left in this size and at this time of the year they tend to go quickly. So if you want to be sure you can get the size we talked about I would really recommend doing a contract for it today. Under our money back guarantee you can always call me and cancel the contract if you change your mind in the next seven days. Is that something you would feel comfortable doing?"

Since it will typically be doves and owls who give you this objection, you will notice that there is lots of reassuring language in the paragraph you just read.

"I Need to Speak to My Husband/Wife/Boss"

This is a very common objection and, in many ways, also the most interesting one. It sounds like the customer is telling us that they are not the only decision maker in this purchase. But what it usually means is that they can make the decision themselves but just don't want to get in trouble for that decision. Keeping that in mind will help us deal with this particular objection in a straightforward way.

By far the most effective way to deal with this objection is to have a policy in place where customers can cancel a contract within a certain number of days and get their money back. A policy like that allows you to close these customers on the spot. But it leaves the door open to them changing their mind, if they do get themselves in trouble over the decision they have made.

If you can't offer them a free annulment of the contract within a limited number of days, then you can also suggest that you speak directly to the other decisionmaker. After all, you don't want anyone else doing your selling for you! It could go something like this:

"I completely understand that you need to speak to your boss before signing the contract, absolutely. We have obviously covered a lot of detail today and in order for her to be able to make a good decision it is probably a good idea that she has a chance to ask me questions just like you have. So, when would be a good time to set up a call with her? Or do you think she would like to come and visit?"

If you take this approach, one of two things will happen.

Either the customer will agree a time where you can speak to the other decisionmaker. If that is the case, you will be one step closer to the sale because you have direct access to the other decisionmaker.

Or if they don't agree a time, chances are they have said this as a stalling tactic. After you suggest to speak directly to the other person they will either give you another objection which is closer to the truth about why they are not ready to sign, or they will find it all to be too much effort and agree to do the contract after all.

Whichever one it is, you are one step closer to the final close.

"I Want to Compare with the Competition Before I Decide"

This one is easy! If your customer wants to shop around, why not make the shopping easy for them? Offer to make them a cup of coffee, seat them in a comfortable chair and hand them an overview of your competition. Have a list ready with the pros and cons of each competitor, with an example of their pricing.

If the customer leaves you to speak with others, you are less likely to get the sale. That is why it is worth putting in some extra effort to keep them engaging with you instead of someone else. Showing them that you are so confident in what you offer that you are willing to tell them all about your competitors is also a strong signal to send the customer.

"It Is Too Expensive"

A few pages ago we looked at 13 different reasons why someone might say this. So, this objection in particular needs to be handled individually depending on why you think the customer feels it is too expensive.

For example, if they are comparing you to storing at their friend's garage then you can highlight all the advantages there are of having professional storage instead of private storage.

The most important thing to remember with this objection is to not take it at face value. Handling this objection well is about understanding what lies beneath it and addressing that, rather than just going straight to a price-based response.

The Doggy Bag on Objections

- o Objection prevention is as important as objection handling.

- o The same objection can have many different underlying reasons. Understanding what they are will make you more effective at handling them.

- o When an objection arises, we go through the steps of the Spiral of Sales again.

- o The most important part of objection handling is to confirm trust with the customer.

- o Replace 'but' with 'and' when you answer a customer's objection.

- o After having answered an objection, always ask your customer if they have other concerns before trying to close them again.

- o Be clear on what your fallback sale is, so that you make the most of every enquiry, even the ones who end up not buying from you.

Discounting

"I think we consider too much the good luck of the early bird and not enough the bad luck of the early worm."

Franklin D. Roosevelt

Who Are Your Discounts Attracting?

There is one question I often see being missed when we are considering which discounts to offer, so we are going to start off with that one.

The purpose of a discount is to attract more customers, so the starting point for any good discount is to ask ourselves: who do we want to attract?

If we offer price discounts, we are likely to attract price sensitive customers who are out for a bargain.

If we discount through adding value, we are likely to attract less price sensitive customers who care more about the overall offering being good.

If we offer prepayment discounts, we will attract a higher proportion of customers who want to stay for longer and who don't have cashflow problems.

If we offer money off for the first few months, we will probably attract more short-staying than long-staying customers.

There are pros and cons with all these customer groups. To keep our business thriving we want to attract customers from each of these segments.

So, any time you are reviewing the discounts you offer, start off by looking at your current discounts and what type of customer you are likely to be attracting with that discount. Are they the customers you want to be attracting? Do the discounts you offer appeal to a variety of customer groups or are you focusing too heavily on one or a few groups? These should be the questions that every discounting decision starts with.

The Good, the Bad and the Ugly

The best discounts are of course the ones that incentivize our customers so much that the discount brings in more business than it costs us. The key to achieving that is to offer something that is low cost to you but has a high perceived value to the customer.

Rent is one example of this, and this is one of the reasons why money off the rent in one form or another is so popular in our industry. Rent has a high perceived value to the customer, but it costs you considerably less to give away.

The bad and the ugly discounts are the ones that cost us more than they bring us, and this is actually far more common than you might think.

To work out if a discount is actually gaining us business, we first need to really know our numbers. We need to know our margins, our average length of stay and how many additional customers the discount attracts.

On the next page you will find a chart that tells you exactly how much more business a discount needs to bring you, in order for it to be worth your while.

Imagine that you offer 50% off the first two months' rent and your average length of stay is 10 months. Over the course of the average customer's rental period with you, that means you are discounting them 10% of the total amount of rent they will pay you.

After your costs are taken out, you have a margin of 25% at your site. What the chart on the next page shows you is that with a 10% discount and a 25% margin, you will need to sell 67% more in order for the discount to bring you the same amount of turnover as you would gain without the discount.

Discount %	Margin %									
	15%	20%	25%	30%	35%	40%	45%	50%	55%	60%
2%	15%	11%	9%	7%	6%	5%	5%	4%	4%	3%
4%	36%	25%	19%	15%	13%	11%	10%	9%	8%	7%
6%	67%	43%	32%	25%	21%	18%	15%	14%	12%	11%
8%	114%	67%	47%	36%	30%	25%	22%	19%	17%	15%
10%	200%	100%	67%	50%	40%	33%	29%	25%	22%	20%
12%	400%	150%	92%	67%	52%	43%	36%	32%	28%	25%
14%	1400%	233%	127%	88%	67%	54%	45%	30%	34%	30%
16%		400%	178%	114%	84%	67%	44%	47%	41%	36%
18%		900%	257%	150%	106%	82%	67%	56%	49%	43%
20%			400%	200%	133%	100%	80%	67%	57%	50%
25%				500%	250%	167%	125%	100%	83%	71%
30%					600%	300%	150%	150%	120%	100%

Need to Read That Again?

Amazing, right? The impact of discounting is greater than most companies and most salespeople realize. So, let's take another example.

This time you are offering the first month at 50% off. Your average length of stay is just under 13 months. That means the discount you are offering on the total rent paid to you over those 13 months is roughly 4%. Your margin is 30%.

Going back to our chart, you would need to sell 15% more because of this discount, in order for it to break even for you. And if you sell more than 15% extra as a result of the discount, then it has been good business for you.

Other Considerations When Discounting

Those were the purely financial aspects of discounting, but of course there are other considerations when you discount. If you are operating in a competitive market, then this is definitely an area where you will need to know what your competitors are offering.

My biggest encouragement to you when looking at your own discounting is to be creative! In some markets, one or two discounts have become the industry norm. Instead of being used as an occasional incentive to bring customers through the door, they have become a permanent feature of selling self-storage.

When that happens, it hurts the whole market. It discounts the value of both our offering and our turnover, without providing us with the gain that discounts are meant to give us; more business.

So be creative! Try different approaches and measure the result. Try different timings, combinations of products and seasonal varieties to work out what your customers respond to the best.

There is no blueprint for what the best discount will be for your unique circumstances. But staying creative and measuring your results is how you make the most of the power that discounting offers when you sell.

The Doggy Bag on Discounting

- o Different discounts will attract different customer groups. Be clear on who you are targeting.

- o To calculate whether a discount is in fact bringing you more turnover, you need to know your average length of stay and your overall margin.

- o Discounts often have a bigger financial impact than we realize, so know yours.

- o The best discounts are the ones that have a low cost to you but have a high perceived value to your customer.

- o Be creative in putting together discounts and measure the results. It will benefit both you and the overall market that you are operating in.

To Stay or to Stray

"Make everything as simple as possible, but not simpler."
Albert Einstein

Congratulations! We have closed the sale with a new customer, and we have done that by adapting to their customer type. We have handled objections along the way, and we have been smart about our discounting. Now, it's time for the next step; to make the time they rent from us a great experience.

In many industries, sales teams and service teams are separated. There is one group that makes the sale and then another group that looks after the customers once they decide to buy. Self-storage is different in that way because most of the time, it is the same people doing the selling and the serving. And let's be clear; that is a great thing.

Most of the skills that we use in sales, we also need in service. We need to read people well, understand their question or problem and then find a good solution together with them.

What I often experience in the self-storage industry is that we try to sell through service. We try to be friendly and helpful and hope that this will help us close the deal. I prefer to turn that principle upside down and instead do service through sales.

By that I mean that we tend to get the most satisfied customers when we apply the principles of selling to our service. That is why the biggest part of this book is about selling; service gets a much smaller page count.

But there are a few differences between service and sales, and we are going to explore those over the next few chapters. Before we do that though, we are going to dive a little deeper into what we mean by service.

What Is Service Actually?

When we serve our customers well, they want to stay with us for longer. They are also more likely to refer us to their friends and family. Put differently, satisfied customers are loyal customers.

This is why it is so important to be clear on what we mean by service. The mental image that people often get when they hear the word 'service' is someone who is over-the-top friendly and helpful.

Being helpful and friendly are part of giving the customer a good experience. But there are actually other factors that play a much bigger role in how loyal our customers are towards us. That is why we are starting our exploration of service by looking a little closer at customer loyalty.

Two Buckets

To understand how customer service affects loyalty, it can be helpful to think of loyalty as two buckets.

In one bucket we pour all the things that make customers loyal. In the other bucket we pour all the things that make customers disloyal.

Starting with the bucket of disloyalty, customer service actually makes up almost all of it.

Yes, you read that right!

The number one thing that drives customers away from businesses is customer service. In fact, customers are four times more likely to leave a service interaction feeling disloyal than loyal to a business.[xiii]

What drives them away isn't the level of friendliness we show them. If they leave us feeling disloyal, it doesn't mean they found us rude or unhelpful. What drives them away is most often the fact that whatever issue they contacted us about, happened in the first place.

So, if negative customer experiences feed a sense of disloyalty with our customers, then it would seem logical that outstanding customer service would do the opposite. Great customer service should feed a sense of loyalty, right?

Wrong!

We can do our best to be friendly and helpful, but if we really want customers to love our business, we need to do more than that.

One major study on customer loyalty followed 75,000 customers over a three-year period, to determine what makes customers loyal or disloyal when they buy.[xiv]

What the researchers found was that a customer's sense of loyalty is actually not that influenced by customer service at all. Service has a fairly small place in the left-hand bucket of loyalty. What takes up the biggest part of that bucket is something completely different. Customers are more loyal when we make it easy for them, when they feel they get good value for money and when they are buying from a brand they can identify with.

That is why, as we explore the anatomy of service over the next few chapters, we are going to look at it in a broader way. We are not going to limit ourselves to just talking about how friendly or helpful we are when we deal with customers. We are going to look at everything that makes a customer want to stay or stray from our site and from our business.

Length of Stay Is Not Length of Loyalty

Length of stay is a common number to measure in any self-storage business and it is an important one. In fact, the most interesting learnings usually come when we look at the average length of stay for different customer groups.

We will usually find that there is a certain age group, a certain post code or a certain marketing source that brings us customers who stay longer. With that knowledge, we can then go out and find more of those customers. So, length of stay is an interesting number to look at when we want to get smarter about our marketing efforts.

It is a less interesting number to look at if we want to measure our customer loyalty. Customers may rent for longer because they just need us for longer, but if a competitor opened up next door, they would be the first to jump ship. Other customers may stay with us only shortly but come back to us the next time they need storage. They might also gladly tell their family and friends to come to us when they need extra space.

This is why we can't use length of stay to measure our customer service and our customer loyalty. Luckily, there is another very simple measurement that can help us do this instead.

The Only Question That Matters

A lot of businesses use customer satisfaction surveys and over time they can tend to get longer and longer, as we add more questions to the mix. That is why I was excited to come across research that had specifically looked at different survey questions to determine which ones actually predict customer loyalty.[xv]

What this research found was that one question is actually enough. There is one single question that predicts loyalty better than any other:

"Would you recommend us to a friend?"

It makes a lot of sense. After all, if a customer is happy enough to recommend us to their family and friends, then our offering and service package as a whole is compelling. If they aren't, then we still have some work to do.

Measuring this response in our site or in our business is the most useful when we track it over time. As a snapshot, it will rarely tell us a lot. But over time, it can tell us which direction we are moving.

Most importantly, it can warn us if we suddenly see a dip. If we notice a downward trend, we have a chance to course correct immediately, instead of having to wait until our financial numbers start spelling it out to us in capital letters.

So, if you haven't been asking your customers this question, now is a great time to start.

The Doggy Bag on Service and Loyalty

- o   Customers are four times more likely to leave a customer service interaction feeling disloyal than loyal.

- o   The biggest driver of loyalty isn't customer service, it is how easy we make the overall experience for our customers.

- o   Length of stay is a good metric for making our marketing more efficient but isn't a good metric for measuring customer loyalty or satisfaction.

- o   Asking customers if they would recommend us to a friend is the most precise way of measuring customer loyalty.

The Steps of Service

"The best way to find yourself is to lose yourself in the service to others."

Mahatma Gandhi

Like we have just seen, good customer service is made up of more than smiling faces and friendly voices. Good customer service is actually about the experience as a whole.

That is why I have put together a separate service model, to help you navigate the different areas you need to consider when you are serving your customers.

The model is called the Steps of Sales and just like our sales model, I would like you to think of these steps more as ingredients you need to create a good service experience, rather than seeing the steps as separate from each other.

Good customer service rests on a foundation of sincerity and trust. Service is good when we make it easy and predictable for our customers and finally, it is when we surprise our customers every once in a while. When we go beyond what they expect of us and create that wow-factor.

The Steps of Service

The easiest way to remember these steps is through the abbreviation:

S incerity
T rust
E ase
P redictability
S urprise

As you can see, each part put together actually forms the word S-T-E-P-S.

Over the next few chapters we are going to dive deeper into this model and look at all the practical ways that we can create a great customer experience while people rent space from us. First on our list is of course sincerity and trust.

Sincerity and Trust

"Listen with curiosity. Speak with honesty. Act with integrity."
Roy T. Bennett

Trust Is Back on the Menu

We have already talked about building trust in the sales process. Continuing to build that trust is a natural and foundational piece of good customer service.

The currency for trust differs from person to person. That is why it is so important that everyone on the team learns about the four customer types and how to adapt their communication style. You may be the most service-minded person with the most helpful intentions. But if you don't communicate that in a way that matches your customer's style, there is a chance you will be misunderstood. Instead of building trust, you could be building quiet frustration instead.

In fact, one mortgage company in the UK trained their entire customer service team on how to adapt their communication to different customer types. They experienced a 40% drop in customer call-backs, simply because customers felt more content after the interaction they had with the team.[xvi]

Two Levels of Sincerity

When we talk about sincerity in customer service, of course it starts with us as people. Our starting point needs to be caring and genuine.

On a very practical level, being sincere with our customers means:

- o It is okay to say we don't know the answer to something.

- o Admit when we have made a mistake.

- o Fix the mistakes we make.

Sincerity also works on a company level and that is true regardless of how big or small your self-storage company is.

Sincerity starts with honoring our commitments and doing what we say we are going to do. But it is also about being true and genuine to our values.

That is why even on a company level, we need to know who we are and what we stand for. That way, every single person in our team will be able to show our customers who we sincerely are as a company.

A big part of showing sincerity and building trust is about being predictable and consistent with our customers. Since we have a whole chapter exploring that topic, we are going to focus here on what to do if that trust is broken or that sincerity is questioned. In other words, what to do if we disappoint our customers.

Finding and Keeping Your Zen

Every once in a while, we encounter customers who are disappointed with us. Sometimes their disappointment is legitimate; we have not lived up to our promise to them.

Other times, their disappointment has little to do with us and our actions. Instead, it is more about their general stress levels. One small thing going wrong by us can be the straw that breaks the camel's back for some customers.

When we are faced with a situation like that, how do we handle it in a way that keeps that trust and shows them sincerity?

Whether the customer's grievance is legitimate or not, the most important thing to bring to a situation like this is calmness. No matter what emotional state our customer is in, our role as customer service professionals is to operate from a state of calmness.

If you do find yourself starting to get agitated by a customer, the quickest way to find your Zen again is to be aware of your breathing. Make your exhales longer than your inhales, as if you were breathing a sigh of relief. It is a simple technique, but it instantly triggers a relaxed response in your nervous system. It helps you find your calm again.

Recycling for Better Relationships

We also need a process that will help us navigate these kinds of situations. Luckily for us, we can recycle a process we already know.

In the section on sales, we talked about how the Spiral of Sales becomes a spiral when we get objections. We talked about how the process for handling an objection contains the same steps as when we make the sale as a whole. Recycling doesn't end there; you can use the same model when you deal with a disappointed customer:

- o Confirm trust by acknowledging their grievance, without necessarily agreeing with the grievance itself.

- o Ask clarifying questions to understand what your customer expected and what kind of solutions the customer might be open to.

- o Suggest a solution and when you do, focus your communication on what you <u>can</u> do for the customer rather than what you can't do.

- o Close the episode by getting your customer to confirm that they are happy with the solution.

In the same way as we can handle objections respectfully and sincerely, we can help disappointed customers by using the exact same formula.

Being Open to Negative Feedback

Being sincere is also about being open to negative feedback. In fact, we should welcome it. Does that feel counter-intuitive?

It shouldn't. If we are genuine and sincere in how we deal with our customers, then of course we want to know if they feel we haven't lived up to their expectations.

Negative feedback can happen even in situations where we have done everything right on paper; for whatever reason, the customer has expected something different than what we have given them.

Some of the feedback we might not be able to do anything about, but negative feedback is a great way to keep learning and keep growing both at a site level and at a company level.

It gives us the chance to correct our course where we need to, and it gives us a chance to manage customer expectations even better.

In order to use negative customer feedback in this way, there needs to be a culture within the team that it's okay to share this kind of feedback. There needs to be respect and understanding amongst everyone that when we get feedback like that, it is not about assigning blame to anyone. It is about looking at how we can learn from the feedback and make future customer interactions even better. If we take that perspective on negative feedback, then it truly is something that we should welcome.

The Doggy Bag on Sincerity and Trust

o Everyone on the team needs to learn about the four customer types and how to adapt their communication style.

o Being sincere is about honoring our commitments and admitting when we don't know something or have made a mistake.

o We can use the same process for dealing with disappointed customers, as we use for handling objections in the sales process.

o If you start feeling agitated by a customer, make your exhale longer than your inhale to trigger a relaxed response in your body.

o Be open to negative feedback and have an understanding within the team that it is okay to share and learn from it.

Ease

"Life is really simple, but we insist on making it complicated."
                                                            Confucius

Slow and Steady Doesn't Win the Race

Think about your own buying habits for a moment. How big a factor is convenience in deciding where and what you buy? Does convenience dictate where you buy your groceries? Does it determine which petrol station you use? Does it decide which online shops you order from?

Convenience has always been a factor for customers, but with so much of our buying happening online, customers are more convenience-driven than ever before.

That is why ease is next in the Steps of Service.

Convenience and ease are areas where our industry has some work left to do. Our administrative processes are often a bit longer than we would like them to be. In general, our customers can also do less online in our industry, than they can in many other industries.

When we are customer facing, there are plenty of processes we can't influence. We can't magic up a customer portal or a smart phone app that will solve our customer's every problem. I would always recommend businesses to develop these tools for their customers, but those decisions and changes happen centrally, for the company as a whole.

That is why we are going to focus here on what we can do to make things easy when we deal with customers on a day-to-day level, regardless of what our processes are or what kind of technology we use.

What we know is that customers love it when we can offer them quick and simple solutions to their problems. When we can't, customers feel like they need to put in unnecessary effort.

So, the interesting question for those of us working in customer service jobs is; what is effort in the eyes of the customer?

What Does Not-Easy Look Like?

The number one thing that customers feel they spend unnecessary effort on is having to contact us more than once about the same thing. In fact, one study found that on average one in five calls are related to a previous problem, not a new one.[xvii]

Do you know what that number is for your site or for your business? If you don't, it could be an interesting number to measure for a while.

As we deal with customers, we should keep this fact at the back of our minds. Anything we can do to avoid giving the customer a reason to contact us more than once about an issue, is worth doing.

For example, if a customer has had an issue with an invoice, we will be doing ourselves a big favor by setting up a reminder when the next invoice gets issued, so that we can manually check it before we send it off.

When we are dealing with hundreds of customers, something like this can seem trivial. But to the customer, it makes a great deal of difference in how they feel about their customer experience with us.

Anticipating the Next Step

Another great way to give the customer a sense of ease and convenience is to always anticipate their next step.

For example, we might find that customers who don't sign up for direct debits are usually late payers the first few months they rent from us. We could be helping both our service and our admin a lot by sending a friendly email a few days before the first or second rent is due:

Hi Sarah,

I see you haven't signed up for direct debit yet. Since you moved in only a few weeks ago, I just wanted to drop you a quick note to say that when your invoice is due in a few days, I'm happy to help if you run in to any questions or queries as you make the payment.

Best wishes,

Martin

Other examples of anticipating the customer's next step could be to give customers a call the day before they are due to move in with us, where we remind them about what they need to bring in order to finalize the contract.

It could even be as simple as having a routine in place where any phone conversation we have with a customer, gets finished off by sending an email to the customer. The email summarizes what we spoke about on the phone, so if the customer was busy or distracted when they spoke to us, they can always go back and reference the email we sent.

Hi Sarah,

Thanks for calling just now. I just wanted to confirm that the move-out notice needs to be sent to us 2 weeks before your expected move-out date. You can fill in the form on our website and I've attached the link to this email, so that you can find it easily when you need it.

If you run in to any questions, you're of course welcome to write or call us.

Best wishes,

Martin

These are just a few simple examples, but there are endless ways we can build up simple routines to anticipate issues for our customers. Through just a few simple processes we can take something that could have been an annoyance and turn it in to a positive and proactive service encounter instead.

Changing the Channel

The last thing on the list of things that customers don't like to do is changing the channel. Here we are not talking about who is in charge of the remote control at home, but about communication channels.

For example, if someone tries to solve an issue through our website but ends up having to call us to resolve it. Or if the customer calls us but ends up having to come by the site to fix something.

If a customer can't solve their issue through the same communication channel they started off in, then it feels like an effort to them. That is why we should always aim to solve the customer's issue within the same channel that they started off contacting us through. To us, it might not feel like an effort to change from email to phone, but to a customer it will.

The Doggy Bag on Ease

- o The biggest driver of customer loyalty is how easy you make it for your customer.

- o Do you know how many of your calls or emails are related to a previous issue and not a new one? If not, it is an interesting number to measure.

- o Reduce the need to contact you more than once about an issue or a question.

- o Anticipate your customer's next step and act on that step before your customer does.

- o Avoid requiring your customer to change communication channels when they are dealing with you about an issue or a question.

Predictability

"Consistency is the true foundation of trust. Either keep your promises or do not make them."

Roy T. Bennett

Speaking with One Voice

Giving our customers a consistent and predictable experience is something that we can't do alone. This next step of predictability can only ever be achieved through a team effort.

Being predictable in how we serve our customers is often translated in to doing the same thing at the same time, over and over again. This is something that to a large extent, our CRM-system will help us achieve. It will generate the letters, invoices and reminders at the right time and help us stay consistent in that way.

But being predictable is also about something that runs much deeper. It is about being consistent in how we communicate. This is an area where, as an industry, we still have some perfecting to do.

In every customer interaction we have, we are showing the customer what kind of company we are. Are we friendly? Are we professional? Are we organized? Are we reliable?

If we want to truly build trust with our customers, we need to speak with one voice in every single customer interaction we have. We need to be consistent in how we communicate, regardless of whether that is an invoice being sent, a late payment phone call or an informative sign by the gate.

Trust requires predictability.

Who Are We?

Before we can communicate in a consistent way, we need to know who we are. We need to know which feelings we want to leave our customers with.

One interesting team exercise to do on this can be for everyone to write down which feelings they think customers should leave you with. When everyone has written these down, compare them with each other. Have you all written the same thing? Are there some differences?

This little exercise can start interesting discussions about who you are as a company and as a team. Once you have all agreed on the list, the team as a whole will be able to deal with customer interactions in a more purposeful way. You will make it easier for everyone to speak with one voice, because you will know what that voice is.

How Do We Show Others Who We Are?

Once the entire team is clear on which impressions you want to leave your customers with, the next team challenge is to go through all the different ways you communicate with your customers and identify places where you are being inconsistent.

Maybe you have a sign that is sending one message, while your website sends another? Maybe your late letters give one impression and your move-out notices a different one?

Ask yourself, as a team, if there is anything you can do to be even more clear about who you are and what you stand for.

For example, if you want to leave your customers feeling like you are friendly and approachable, then you might want to finish off emails with the name of the person writing the email instead of signing it with a generic team name.

The Last Step Is the Next Step

One of the principles we talked about in the sales section is also useful when we want to give our customers a predictable experience.

When we are selling, we finish off one step of the sales process by telling the customer what the next step will be. In service, we do the same thing.

If we are calling a customer to remind them that they are late with their payment, the last part of our call could be:

"If you don't manage to make the payment in the next few days like we've just spoken about, then we will send you a formal reminder letter once you are 12 days late. Once that letter is sent we do add a late fee to your account, to cover the admin costs we have for sending out the reminders. Just so you are aware what comes next."

Relationships with customers are built when we consistently delivering on our promises. So, whenever we can we should be explicit about what comes next. After that, we show the customer that we do exactly what we have said we are going to do. That is how we build loyalty and trust through predictability, one small step at a time.

The Doggy Bag on Predictability

○ Predictability requires everyone on the team to speak with one voice.

○ Be clear on which feelings and impressions you want to leave your customers with.

○ Review all the ways you communicate with your customers and highlight places where you are not sending consistent signals.

○ Finish off every customer interaction by telling them what the next step is going to be.

Surprise

"Whoever can surprise well must conquer."
John Paul Jones

That Little Box

Imagine that you are in the middle of moving from one home to another. You have finally packed the whole truck up with stuff, you head down to the storage facility with a group of friends to put your stuff in storage and by this point you are already pretty beat. You have been up later than usual for the past few weeks getting everything ready and this morning you had to rush through breakfast to fit in final preparations for the big move.

You get to the storage facility and everyone is starting to feel a bit hungry and tired from the busy morning. You find your unit, open the door and notice something inside. It is a small moving box with a few bottles of water and some snacks, together with a hand-written note from the storage team wishing you good luck on moving day.

This is just one example of how surprises can be used to put the icing on the cake of the customer experience. This example is for movers, but you can build other surprises for business customers or long-term private storage customers too.

The great thing about surprises is they don't need to be complicated or cost a lot. It truly is the thought that counts. It is often the little touches, like the hand-written note, that makes it memorable and impactful.

What Makes A Surprise Special?

The more personal a surprise is, the bigger an impression it will make. An auto-generated, templated and colorful email from the system wishing your customer a happy birthday is going to make much less of an impression than a hand-written card.

So, the key to making your surprises both impactful and economical is to make them personal. It also means that your creativity is your only limitation!

Surprise by Teamwork

As you start planning your customer surprises, it is an excellent opportunity to build relationships with other local businesses. For example, there may be a local hairdresser, massage therapist, or florist who would happily give you a stack of discount vouchers, so that you can pass them on to your customers as part of a surprise.

Imagine being a customer who has just moved out. The day after you have emptied your unit, you get a card in the mail that says:

Hi Beth,

I just wanted to personally say thank you for storing with us. We've loved having you with us for the past 5 months. Emptying a storage unit can be hard work, so I have included a 10% off discount voucher to Sandy's Massages down the road. That way, you can treat yourself to a foot rub when you feel you need one. I've also thrown in a few referral cards. If you ever hear of family and friends that need storage, we are of course happy to help them just as we have helped you.

All the best of luck in your new home,

Adrian and Fiona

And who knows, maybe now that you are giving out promotional but value-adding vouchers for a local business, that business might feel inclined to hand out your vouchers to their customers. You could quite easily find yourself both marketing and building customer surprises, without it adding any real cost to you.

The Surprise Calendar

Surprises should surprise your customer, but they shouldn't surprise you. You will need a system or a calendar of some kind that will remind you of which customer needs a surprise when, so they happen consistently for everyone who stores with you.

Customers usually have the most contact with us around the time they move in, and then again when they move out. That is why these are two excellent times to build in some kind of surprise to your customer experience. It will leave your customer with a strong first and last impression.

Apart from the move-in and move-out surprises, your surprise calendar should contain one or two more contact points during a year. This can be a phone call, a written note or even an email. It can be as simple as a birthday greeting, a Christmas card, or a phone call just to check that everything is running smoothly and they don't have any questions or issues.

A surprise calendar like this will add enough icing on the cake of your customer service to leave people with that wow-factor we want to create. At the same time though, it is also manageable both from a time and money point of view.

Once we have perfected our customer surprises, we have mastered all the ingredients we need to create a great service experience. We have taken all the Steps of Service and allowed them to come together. As a whole, these steps offer our customers the sense that we are reliable, caring, and even a little fun!

The Steps of Service

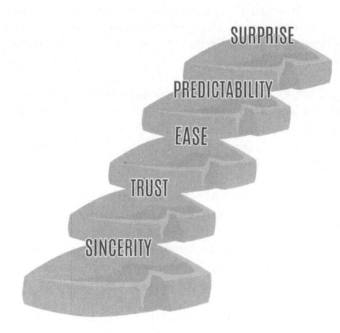

The Doggy Bag on Surprises

- o   Surprises add a wow-factor to the customer experience.

- o   The more personal you can make your surprise, the more impactful it will be.

- o   Creating customer surprises is an excellent opportunity to network with other local businesses.

- o   You will need a calendar or system to remind you about who should be surprised when.

- o   The ideal surprise calendar includes one at move-in and move-out respectively, plus one or two additional touch points during a year.

Growing

"Life shrinks or expands in proportion to one's courage."
Anais Nin

We have now covered all the things you can do to make the most of every customer interaction you have, whether that is when you are selling or while the customer is renting from you. You now know everything you need to become successful at both sales and service.

Our final stop for this book is to look at what it takes to stay successful; how to stay at the cutting edge of what you do.

Learning from Bill Gates and Rain Worms

Bill Gates reads about 50 books every year. He has wealth beyond measure and is at a point in his life where he could lean back and take it easy. So why does he read so much? In his own words: "I both learn new things and test my understanding".[xviii]

In one study that spanned a five-year period, Tom Corley looked at the habits of financially successful people. What he found was that 88% of people with financial success read at least 30 minutes a day. 63% listen to audiobooks on their way to and from work, and it probably won't surprise you that fiction isn't at the top of their reading list.[xix]

Staying curious and staying open to new ideas, new perspectives and new approaches is how we stay successful over time.

Learning can take many forms. Reading or listening to audiobooks is one way. Another way is to take courses, either online or in person. Being coached and getting feedback from others around us is especially effective at highlighting where we might have 'blind spots' in our own approaches to sales and service. Maybe there are things that we aren't noticing about our own approach that someone else would be able to make us aware of in the blink of an eye.

And then there is of course the oldest form of learning; trial and error. Trial and error has been a learning method for creatures of all sizes since the beginning of time; even rain worms use trial and error.

We can use trial and error in sales and service by taking that input that we get from books, courses, colleagues and coaches to try different approaches. The key to using trial and error successfully is to have a solid way of measuring our results when we do.

If you approach a trial and error experiment in the right way, it will be able to tell you exactly which approach works best for you and for your customers.

No matter which route you take to continuous learning, the lesson here is to stay curious and to stay open-minded. To have a starting point that says there is always more we could be learning, there is always more we could be challenging.

Goal!

Now let's for a moment dial the clock back a little to 1979. A group of fresh-faced university graduates were asked by researchers at Harvard Business School if they had any clear, written goals for their future and whether they had made plans to accomplish those goals.[xx]

> 3% had written goals and plans.

> 13% had goals, but these goals weren't in writing.

> 84% had no explicit goals.

Time went by and ten years later, researchers checked in with the same group of graduates to see how they were doing.

It turned out that the 3% who had written goals were earning, on average, ten times as much as the other 97% combined! Yes, you read that right. Ten times!

This study only looked at success from the point of view of income and of course success is about a lot more than money. But the study still carries an important lesson about how powerful written goals can be.

Does that mean we can set ourselves a wild goal, scribble it down on a napkin and then wait for it to happen? Of course not. What made the 3% so successful is probably what they went through in order to be able to write those goals down in the first place.

They had to be clear on what they wanted and which steps they needed to take to get there. In order to be able to write down their goal, they needed clarity both about the goal itself and about the road they needed to travel towards it.

You may have heard the phrase 'smart goals', which refers to this acronym:

S pecific

M easurable

A chievable

R ealistic

T ime-limited

Goals can take many forms and don't need to be financial at all. Your goal could be to read a certain number of books. It could be to increase your conversion rate or to reach a certain level of occupancy.

Whichever goal you set yourself, make it smart. Make it specific enough that you can measure whether or not you have reached it. Make it achievable and realistic, so that you stay motivated. And make it time-limited so you can plan which steps you need to take every single week in order to get to where you want to be.

Pressure Points

Remember at the beginning of the book, I talked about how growth happens when we pay attention to the small details? How the way to create a great thing is to get the small things right?

Each business has their own pressure points for growth, but there are six pressure points that are universal to all self-storage companies:

- o Number of Enquiries
- o Conversion Rate
- o Average Length of Stay
- o Average Rent per Unit
- o Margins
- o Income from Extras

These six pressure points represent areas in any self-storage business that have a direct impact on the results we are creating.

If we generate more enquiries but everything else stays the same, we will be better off because in total, we will end up with more sales.

If our conversion rate improves, we will convert more of those enquiries into customers and end up with even more sales, and so on.

When you work with sales and service in a self-storage facility, you can directly impact four out of these six pressure points; conversion rate, average length of stay, average rent per unit and income from extras.

By mastering your sales skills, you can grow your conversion rate and make the value of each and every transaction or invoice as high as possible. Through the service you offer you can grow your length of stay.

Depending on the size of the company you work in, you might not be able to influence the number of enquiries or the margins a lot. But even if that is the case, it still leaves you with four out of six universal pressure points for business growth that are resting in your hands.

After having read this book, you have a range of tools and techniques that will help you nurture and grow these pressure points in your own site, and through that for the whole business. Put differently, you now have enough small things to go out and create a great thing.

So, go create! Translate all these words into action; action that is adapted to your market, to your customers and to your own personal style. Accumulate those actions consistently over time and you will see your very own 'great thing' take shape. You will see your trajectory starting to change.

The Doggy Bag on Growing

- o Stay curious and stay open-minded through continuous learning.

- o Set smart goals for yourself.

- o Working in sales and service, you directly influence four out of the six universal pressure points for growth in the business.

- o It's time to start building your great thing and start changing your own trajectory. So, stop reading this book and start doing.

About Christel F. Land

Christel was born in Sweden in 1979 to a Danish mother and an American father. She has also lived in Germany, the UK and China and as a consequence speaks a handful of languages.

She holds a B.Sc. in Economics and International Studies from the London School of Economics and a Master of Business Administration from the University of Leicester.

Christel became a certified business coach in 2008 and has since also qualified in mBIT coaching, a neuroscience based coaching technique. Today she teaches coaching internationally.

She entered the self-storage industry in 2002 and worked for 7 years in what was then one of the largest pan-European chains. She has also spent 5 years as Project Manager and later Managing Director for a supplier of IT systems to the self-storage industry.

Christel specializes in working with smaller and medium-sized businesses, both within and beyond the self-storage industry. Today, she splits her time between coaching businesses to grow, running training courses, authoring books, and speaking at conferences and events.

Her company Clover Four ApS is registered in Denmark, where she lives with her family. For more information about Christel, you can visit her website at **www.cloverfour.eu** or contact her by email: **cland@cloverfour.eu**

Legal stuff

The materials and information in this publication are provided as is, without representation, endorsement or warranty (express or implied) of any kind. This publication is designed to provide accurate and authoritative information about the subject matter covered, and best attempts have been made to provide the most accurate and valid information, but the publisher and author does not warrant that the information is incomplete or free from inaccuracies.

This publication contains ideas, opinions, tips and techniques for improving sales and service performance in self-storage businesses. The accuracy and completeness of the information provided herein, and the opinions stated herein are not guarantees, not warranties to or towards the production of any particular result, and the advice and strategies contained herein may not be suitable for every individual or every business.

You read this publication with the explicit understanding that neither the publisher nor the author shall be liable for any direct or indirect loss of profit or any other commercial damages, including but not limited to special, incidental, punitive, consequential or other damages. In reading or using any part or portion of this publication, you agree to not hold, not attempt to hold the publisher and author liable for any loss, liability, claim, demand, damage and all legal costs or other expenses arising whatsoever in connection with the use, misuse or inability to use the materials. In jurisdictions that exclude such limitations, liability is limited to the consideration paid by you for the right to view or use these materials, and/or the greatest extent permitted by law.

Publications by Christel F. Land

"The Cutting Edge of Self-Storage" is a series of three books so far. Sales and Service and The Growth Handbook are published in the autumn of 2019 and Marketing in the spring of 2020.

The aim of the series is to bring together the most relevant research, best practices and industry know-how to offer cutting edge perspective on how we can excel at sales and marketing in our self-storage businesses.

If you have enjoyed this book or any of the other titles, please do leave a review on Amazon. It will help others like you find this book as they search for information and inspiration for their business.

Publications about decision making

A rhyming children's book that uses the principles of mBIT coaching to teach children how to make values-based decisions.

Publications about autism

The Superhero Brain
Explaining Autism to
Empower Kids

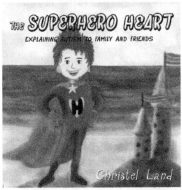

The Superhero Heart
Explaining Autism to
Family and Friends

Superhero Guts
An Everyday Poem for
Special Needs Parents

Online Sales Training with Christel F. Land

If you would like to take a sales course with Christel, you can of course invite her to run a course for your team. But if that doesn't work for you, you can also take part in the online sales training she has put together.

Spread across 16 different modules, it contains practical tools and techniques for how to sell self-storage. It also has lots of practical exercises along the way, to help you adapt the material to your own site.

The course is only available through self-storage associations, so if you are interested get in touch with your self-storage association about getting access to the course.

References

These are references to specific studies that are cited in this book.

[i] Sam Page, "Digital Neuromarketing", 2015

[ii] David Hoffeld, "The Science of Selling", 2016

[iii] Covey, Stephen M.R., "The Speed of Trust: The One Thing That Changes Everything", 2006

[iv] Sam Page, "Digital Neuromarketing", 2015

[v] Matthew Dixon and Brent Adamson, "The Challenger Sale", 2011

[vi] John M Grohol, "Weather Can Change Your Mood", PsychCentral 2019

[vii] John Staughton, "Can Humans Actually Multitask?", ScienceABC 2016

[viii] "B2B's Digital Revolution", https://www.thinkwithgoogle.com/marketing-resources/b2b-digital-evolution

[ix] Sam Page, "Digital Neuromarketing", 2015

[x] Sam Page, "Digital Neuromarketing", 2015

[xi] Brian Tracey, "The Psychology of Selling", 2004

[xii] Beverly Kepple, "DISCovering the ultimate tool", 2010

[xiii] M. Dixon, K. Freeman, N. Toman, "Stop Trying to Delight Your Customers", Harvard Business Review on Increasing Customer Loyalty, 2011

xiv M. Dixon, K. Freeman, N. Toman, "Stop Trying to Delight Your Customers", Harvard Business Review on Increasing Customer Loyalty, 2011

xv F. F. Reichheld, "The One Number You Need to Grow", Harvard Business Review on Increasing Customer Loyalty, 2011

xvi M. Dixon, K. Freeman, N. Toman, "Stop Trying to Delight Your Customers", Harvard Business Review on Increasing Customer Loyalty, 2011

xvii M. Dixon, K. Freeman, N. Toman, "Stop Trying to Delight Your Customers", Harvard Business Review on Increasing Customer Loyalty, 2011

xviii Carrie M. King, "Bill Gates Reads 50 Books A Year – Find Out Why", Blinkist Magazine Apr 20 2018

xix Tom Corley, "Change Your Habits, Change Your Life", 2016

xx Annabel Acton, "How To Set Goals (And Why You Should Write Them Down), Forbes.com Nov 3 2017